HOVEL IN THE HILLS

'Do-it-yourself enthusiasts will be enthralled by Elizabeth West's opening chapters on gadgetry and botchery at Hafod, the "hovel" of her book. Even I, who hurry uncomprehendingly away from a chisel or a plane enjoy them, though I resented them on reaching the chapters on gardening and birds.

So exquisite were these that I wanted a bookful, and found it difficult to accept that a woman who could write so beautifully about the song of a curlew could have been a typist at Bristol, engaged peripherally on the construction of the evil-sounding Concorde.

Mrs West writes with sensitivity, compassion, and delightful humour . . . She and her husband have achieved the life they sought, working in domestic service in winter to support their subservient summers at Hafod, but one hopes fervently that, having produced this book, Elizabeth will not allow the "simple" life to stifle her writing talent.'

BIRMINGHAM MAIL

Also by Elizabeth West

GARDEN IN THE HILLS
KITCHEN IN THE HILLS

and published by Corgi Books

Elizabeth West

Hovel in the Hills

an account of 'the simple life'

CORGI BOOKS

HOVEL IN THE HILLS

A CORGI BOOK 0 552 10907 X

First published in Great Britain by
Faber & Faber Ltd.

PRINTING HISTORY
Faber edition published 1977
Corgi edition published 1978
Corgi edition reprinted 1979 (twice)
Corgi edition reprinted 1980
Corgi edition reprinted 1981
Corgi edition reprinted 1983

This book is set in Plantin 10/11pt

Corgi Books are published by Transworld Publishers Ltd.,
Century House, 61-63 Uxbridge Road,
Ealing, London W5 5SA.
Made and printed in Great Britain by
Hunt Barnard Printing Ltd., Aylesbury, Bucks.

Yng nghennau'r sach mae cynilo
(The time to economize is when
the flour sack is first opened)

All events in this book are true, but a few
place-names have been changed and locations
'moved'. The characters in Chapters 12 and
13 are fictitious.

Some of the material in Chapter 5 has appeared in
The Countryman and my thanks are due to the Editor
for his kind permission to reprint.
  I am also grateful to Lever Brothers Limited
for allowing me to quote passages from *Good Plain
Cookery* and *The Economical Housewife*.

This account covers the period of our lives from 1965
to 1974.

Elizabeth West   *Hafod, 1977*

FOREWORD *by John Seymour*

Working on the assumption (and it is only an assumption) that we have one life each it is important to every one of us that we do the best we can with it. If society says to us: 'We are prepared to look after you from the cradle to the grave provided you live in a boring place and work at a boring job' then we should consider very seriously whether this is a bargain we want to accept. The author of this book has declined to accept it, and she is one of a growing number of people who have decided not to make this bargain. In the first place, she and her husband answered the question of 'Where shall we live?' not with the answer: 'We will have to live where our work is' but with the answer: 'We will live in a beautiful place of our own choosing.'

People who do this are always asked by their friends: 'Yes—but what will you do to earn a living?' Now the only way to answer that question is by going and finding out. I have come in contact now with some hundreds of people who have made this choice, a choice that would have been unthinkable to all but a tiny minority of people twenty years ago, and I have been impressed time after time at the enormous variety of ways that such people have solved the problem of making a living in the place of their choice. True the Wests have had to go away from home from time to time—but there is nothing wrong with this; it is a perfectly happy way to live to sally forth from your secure home from time to time to bring back the mutton, as it were: sailors, fishermen, drovers, traders, pirates, brigands, and soldiers of fortune, travelling actors, explorers; countless people of great initiative and resourcefulness have done just this.

But what has surprised me is how so many of these people who have fled from what they thought was a corrupt and corrupting urban society, have arrived in their Shangri-las either with no idea of how they were going to earn a living, or else with an idea which has proved in practice to be the wrong one: and found—quite unexpectedly and somehow almost without looking for it—a solution that they would never have dreamed of. The fact is, there is a livelihood for people in the country—ay and in the remote fastness of Wales too—just as much as there is in the middle of Birmingham. There *is* a livelihood, for any people with determination and initiative—and the sort of people who refuse to accept the dull bargain society offers are always such people—in any part of the countryside you like to find. You may have to go away sometimes—but you go away to come back again. And I wouldn't mind betting that the Wests, when they get tired of making forays into the outer world, will find a perfectly acceptable way of earning at home the little money that even the self-supporter needs.

Bee-keeping; designing and selling a range of picture postcards; publishing a series of small guides to the countryside; making wooden soup bowls on a lathe; building boats; making violins, spinning wheels, jewellery, leather objects; potting; weaving; engraving on slate; doubling as a landscape artist and a fisherman; illustrating botanical treatises; running a craft shop; running a second-hand tool shop; dentistry; doing fencing on contract; painting shop and van signs; jobbing building; nursery gardening; market gardening; sheep shearing: these are just a few of the solutions to this problem of earning a living *where you want to live* among people I know closely in my immediate vicinity that spring to mind without thinking about it very much. It would surprise me if a quarter of the people practising the above trades had thought of their particular trade when they made the plunge into self-sufficient living in the country. And the point is that few of them would be able to live at these trades if they had to pay urban rents and buy their food at the supermarket.

The countryside *needs* such people. As well as the commercial farmers and farm workers we need people who practise

8

a thousand trades—and people with fun and laughter in their hearts, and the sort of courage and initiative the Wests have got. And there is more at stake than our own happiness and amusement. Our very existence as a species may depend on our getting more people with brains and imagination back on the land again; to grow the food that will be needed desperately to feed us all when the oil runs out, or when civilization as we know it now runs down out of sheer boredom and frustration, as it looks like doing.

For two hundred years now the cities have been sucking the life blood out of the countryside. Intelligent country boys and girls have inevitably been drawn to the big city, and, except for occasional holidays, they have not come back again. Now big-city culture is being examined closely, and is being found wanting. There are a million unemployed people in this country now, who knows how many there will be in five years' time? More young men and women are opting out of it: some of them negatively, living on charity and the handouts of urban society, but some—like the Wests—positively, determined to claim their birthright of their own countrysides and be worthy of it, to build good and secure homes there and take their proper places as full members of country society. There is a great renaissance going on. The flood of brains and imagination from the country to the cities is being stemmed—and a gradually increasing trickle is running in the opposite direction. The pioneers of this reverse movement may have felt it lonely and tough going at first, but as more and more people like the Wests move out—*drop in* as we should call it—so we shall give each other more mutual support, life will be fuller, and city people will have to come to the country if they want to see where it's all happening.

CONTENTS

1. WE TAKE TO THE HILLS

'Your *what*?' said Alan. 'My brassière straps,' I repeated. 'They're caught up in the mangle again.'

With the air of a man born to shoulder many burdens, he accompanied me to the mangle house. Why-don't-you-get-yourself-liberated-and-save-us-both-a-lot-of-trouble was the general drift of his comments as he eased the twisted straps from the snarl-up around the oily cogs.

Later, whilst hopefully dabbing at grease-caked broderie Anglaise, I reflected upon the problems of washday in the wilderness. And it occurred to me that I am possibly the only woman in Britain whose washing is liable to end up dirtier than it started.

There are compensations however. We are so isolated up here that my tattered array of patched sheets, darned woollies, frayed towels and threadbare knickers is viewed only by the odd passing raven. And they just *kronk* disbelievingly and hurry away.

I had better explain where 'up here' is. Come with me to North Wales ...

Between the high, wild moorland of Hiraethog and the lush green lowlands of the Conwy Valley, lies a scrubby rock-strewn wilderness clothed in bracken, gorse and ancient haw-thorns. This untamed land is criss-crossed by lanes running between walls of moss-covered boulders, edged by foxgloves and gouged deep by centuries of plodding feet. One of the lanes, four miles long and looping high to skirt the moor, is rough and unsurfaced. A few ruined cottages stand alongside it. Their roofs have long since collapsed, their windows are blank and the stones of their walls are slipping outwards.

Huddling against the boulder-strewn hillside they cannot easily be seen from a distance. Rowan and blackthorn grow on their thresholds and grass clings to their chimney stacks. The moor is reclaiming them.

One of the cottages is not yet a ruin. The roof has been patched up, cement has been trowelled into the cracks of the walls and the windows have been renewed. This is where we live, Alan and I. The place is called Hafod.

We own this cottage with its cluster of outbuildings and one steeply sloping field that rises to 1,050 feet behind us. The perimeter of our land is marked by a boundary bank topped with a fence of oak posts and five strands of wire. The fence, we are told, is fifty years old. The oak posts are still hard, but fissured and withered. Some of them float freely from the ground and hang between the wires. We started to repair the fence a few years ago with new larch posts. But the larch posts are beginning to rot and a few have snapped off. The old fence looks much the same now as it did when we arrived, except that there are now larch, as well as oak, posts hanging on the wires.

Our land is separated from the lane by a straggling neglected hedge. We are trying to improve the hedge by cutting and laying the hawthorn, and sowing acorns in the gaps. One large gap is filled by a mattress spring. A mattress spring makes an excellent stop gap. New growth of hawthorn and bramble can be woven between the wires making a strong windproof screen. A chaffinch once built her nest there—the neat mossy cup being held firmly between the wire coils.

In our field we have a small boggy patch growing rushes and mosses, a high wild ridge of rollicking gorse, and a rocky spur where pink-tinged English stonecrop carpets the ground and where rabbits chase around a solitary rowan. The rowan, old and leaning, wears tiny leaves and miniature red berries at the end of its brittle grey branches. We fear that one day it must fall, and after every gale we peer anxiously up the hill from the back door. We are always relieved to see it still there, stiff and creaking on the skyline.

Near the rowan amongst the rocks we have sitting places, and from these we view our horizon. Only three occupied homesteads are in sight—the nearest being that of our neighbour, a mile or so away. The moorland tumbles gently away in front of us in a great sea of bracken, gorse and rushes reaching down to the valley, which is out of our sight. On the other side of the valley the land rises in gently rounded hills, patchworked with small fields and woods, and laced with stone walls. A Forestry Commission woodland broods upon Moel Penybryn. Behind the hills the rocky peaks of the mountains soar into the sky.

From our sitting place up by the old rowan we see spread out in front of us the whole range of mountains from the Arrans in the south, the Moelwyns due south-west, to the Carneddau in the north-west. The graceful queenly slopes of Moel Siabod dominate our landscape, with a shoulder of Yr Wyddfa nudging her from behind, and the ridge of Tryfan arching to her right.

In summertime it is a tranquil scene, with the shadows of the clouds scudding across the hills and the faraway bleating of sheep and the singing of larks. In winter it is silent and majestic, with every ridge, slope and shoulder shawled in white. But this becomes an enchanted place at the time of a midsummer sunset, when the mountains stand out sharply against the orange and turquoise radiance behind, and the curlews call hauntingly from the marshlands. Then we are speechless with awe. There are feelings inside us that could only be expressed in poetry, but we haven't the words. So we watch in silence.

What are we doing here? On hot sunny days you will find us, dressed in shorts, working outside. Alan will be stripped to the waist. It is quite obvious that we do not belong here. No self-respecting Welsh hill farmer takes off his shirt out of doors, and I have yet to see a Welsh woman wearing shorts. (Mind you, I've yet to see one wearing red flannel and a high hat! The national costume around here is a large floral pinny and wellington boots.) On cold wet days you will probably find us in the kitchen. Depending upon the time of day and year, you will find me washing up, making bread, ironing, bottling fruit, boiling up jam on the Primus or watching Alan at work. He will be sitting cross-legged on the floor surrounded by parts of a bicycle, clock, gun, electric fire, branding iron, adding machine, or whatever the current thing brought in for repair happens to be. Or he may be smoking his pipe and watching me at work.

We will greet you with a smile and a slightly selfconscious '*Bore da*' if we think you are a local. And a suspicious 'Good morning' if we can tell that you aren't. Our accents are of the West Country.

We moved to Hafod from Bristol in 1965, and cannot now remember whose idea it was. We take it in turns to blame each other, or congratulate ourselves, depending upon whether it has been a good day spent picking sun-ripened raspberries, or a bad day replacing slates that were torn off in last night's gale. All I know is that a life of primitive isolation was not what I had in mind at the time we got married. I don't know about Alan. You can never tell with him.

'Ah, you're getting out of the rat race,' our friends said knowingly when we told them. We didn't argue. It was easier to let the cliché stand. I am not sure that I know what the rat race is—or whether in fact I ever qualified to have been in it. There was no one breathing menacingly at my shoulder desirous of snatching my job as typist with the British Aircraft Corporation, and there were certainly no dizzy heights for me to claw my way up to in the Typing Pool. I cycled to work each day, with my bread and cheese sandwiches in my saddle-bag, and shared an office with some pleasant girls with whom I exchanged knitting patterns and gossip. Alan's life as an accounting machine mechanic was, perhaps, more trying. His job was to install these complex high-priced machines in the offices of people who did not really need them, but who had been persuaded to buy them—and then to go back to put them right when they had gone wrong, and try to explain why. 'Well, if you *will* buy such bloody rubbish what can you expect!' is an explanation hardly likely to please either customer or employer. But then, Alan has never been particularly concerned about pleasing his employer. Not long before he left them Alan's employers decided to improve the status of the workshop staff by calling them 'Field Engineers' and inviting them to accept a monthly salary paid by cheque direct into a bank account. The effect upon the workshop was instantaneous. New suits began to appear, and one or two briefcases. One man abandoned his *Daily Mirror* in favour of carrying *The Times*. The firm were delighted at the way all the 'Field Engineers' responded to their new image. All except one man, that is. Alan, invoking the Truck Act and demanding to be paid weekly in 'coins of the realm', remained a defiant mechanic and started riding his bicycle to work. The firm were no doubt extremely relieved when he resigned.

If we were not conscious of being in a rat race we were certainly aware of the pointlessness of much of our days' activities. We were both spending a lot of time doing things that seemed to have nothing to do with living. At the end of a day spent typing columns of figures that had some remote connection with the production of Concorde, all I had achieved was a foggy head and double vision. To spend all day indoors working a machine in order to earn money to buy food seemed a daft way of carrying on when, with a re-organization of our lives, I could be enjoying myself out of doors producing some of that food myself. Give me a vegetable patch and a few hens to look after and I could be content.

I am not sure whether Alan's dream involved quite so much hard work as mine. His idea of the country life was, I think, leaning upon the garden fence watching the homeward flight of geese, or sitting with his tankard on a bench outside the local pub.

But there was another ambition that we shared (if ambition is the right word for it): a sneaky and entirely unmeritorious desire to cast off the shackles of regular employment. To be employed upon pointless and unsatisfying work is quite bearable if you have agreed to do it for a certain limited time and if, at the end of that period, you collect your wages and you are free. In this way the worker can retain his dignity. He has sold his services, but not his soul. In the 1960s it wasn't necessary for man and wife to work five days a week all year round in order to maintain a roof over their heads and sufficient food in their bellies. The fact that most of our friends *did* work five days a week all year round was due to two

17

reasons. Firstly they wanted a lot more than the basic necessities of life. They wanted the best house they could possibly afford to mortgage, a car, television set, new furnishings that were changed frequently and expensive hobbies. Secondly, the casual worker is not liked by employers. An employer prefers his workers to be firmly shackled by paid holidays, sick-benefit, welfare schemes, sports clubs and pension schemes.

Having said that, it must be admitted that some of our friends actually liked their jobs—incredible though it seemed to us. And a cage is only a prison to someone who wants to get out of it.

At the time of our marriage we were dutiful slaves of The System. We were both firmly manacled to secure jobs and wrapped up in various hobbies. Alan's contribution to our first home was a lot of expensive photographic equipment, his cycle, a sailing dinghy and a twelve-seater Utilabrake. My dowry consisted of books and stereophonic record-playing equipment.

It took us only a few months to sort out our values. We decided that we did not want a new semi-detached house, a car, a television set, nor expensive furnishings; and our hobbies were only palliatives to a way of life that was becoming more and more pointless. The thing we both wanted, and were noticeably short of, was time. Time to think; time to ponder upon what life was all about. Now, if we paid cash for a small primitive cottage and a patch of land we would surely have the basics for a simple life that would not need a very high income to maintain. As every countryside community needs its van drivers, road menders, postmen, car mechanics and shop assistants, we felt confident that we could pick up some form of employment, it did not really matter what. If you have a roof over your head, vegetables in the garden and everything paid for—then you can chop and change jobs and survive periods of unemployment without worrying too much.

It was still possible to buy cottages for well under £2,000, and if we lived upon my wages and banked Alan's we could probably save up enough money in a couple of years. Once we were in possession of this cottage and bit of land we should be free—free to choose our way of life. Should we become itinerants, travelling around the roads of Britain doing odd jobs, and returning to hibernate each winter in our cottage? Or should we work the holiday season at a seaside camp? Or should we stay put and cultivate a market garden? The important thing was to get a rural base; a patch of land that was ours and a simple cottage. Then we could sit by our fireside and work out a way of life that made some sort of sense.

Alan sold his dinghy and the Utilabrake and we started saving his wages. We spent money only upon essentials, and for the next couple of years I cycled to work wearing the same clothes almost every day. (When it came to giving me a 'leaving present' my friends in the office were in two minds whether it should be a book token or a new skirt!) We were, however, buying tools, equipment and clothes that we thought we should need in our future life of peasantry. Now was the time to buy them, we decided, whilst we still had the money and the opportunity. Today, when almost everything is high priced and of inferior quality we are extremely glad that we took this early decision. Surprisingly enough—bearing in mind that at the time we did not know what sort of life lay ahead— we made very few mistakes in these early purchases. As things have turned out only two items proved to be of no use—a long-handled brushing hook and an all-weather coat. I don't know what sort of a giant could effectively trim hedges with a long-handled brushing hook but, for all the success Alan had, he might as well have been bashing at the hawthorn with a boiler stick. The hook, heavy and unwieldy and shaped like a hockey stick, seemed more likely to decapitate the hedger's assistant than trim the hedge, so it lay unused in the stable for a few years until eventually we persuaded a local iron-monger to swap it for a billhook. We have not been able to dispose of the coat like this. Triple-breasted, multi-buttoned, belted, strapped and looped, it was guaranteed to protect the wearer from the fiercest blizzard. Perhaps it does—we don't know. What the guarantee did not say was that once the wearer was buttoned, belted, strapped and looped into the garment he could not move! So the all-weather (and very expensive) coat now hangs on a nail in an outhouse, dusty, mouse-nibbled and unused.

After two and a half years, and with just over £2,000 in the bank, we felt that the time had come for a positive move. The sort of property we wanted, and could afford, would have to be on or near wild, open country, and we decided to confine our search to Dartmoor, Exmoor and Wales. We sent a circular letter to a list of west country estate agents, advertised in two Welsh newspapers, and then sat back and waited for the cottages to come tumbling through the letter-box.

The next few months were fun. Admittedly most of the estate agents took no notice of our requirements and sent us every crumbling ruin and unlikely mansion that they had on their books, but reading through all the effusive descriptions just added to our entertainment. Our circular letter had made it quite clear that we were looking for a cottage with a minimum of five rooms, preferably with a footpath approach, and a couple of acres of land. Mains services were not required, and £2,200 was the top limit. Yet we were sent details of small hotels, modern bungalows and even a nineteenth-century mock abbey going for £9,000.

However, one Devon estate agent understood exactly what we wanted, and sent us information on several properties that were so interesting we hired a vehicle and drove down to have a look at them. But although we liked them all, each had an insurmountable snag. One single-storey cottage going with six acres of woodland was in a deep valley with a torrential stream a bit too close for comfort; a wooden cabin high in the woods near Exford had only a very small garden which was completely hemmed in by trees. A cottage on Dartmoor, mentioned in the Domesday Book, had a twisting secret staircase behind the fireplace that charmed us, but a peculiar neighbour who didn't. 'Ivy-in-the-Dell'—a tiny cob and thatch cottage in North Devon priced at £1,200, separated from the road by two fields and going with three acres of land, seemed just the right place according to the agent's particulars. But we found that it squatted in a deep squelching saucer—the cob walls soaking up all the excess moisture squeezed out of the surrounding sloping fields. 'Ivy-in-the-Dell' had become a sog-in-the-hollow, and was rapidly disintegrating.

Our advertisements in the Welsh newspapers brought us only four replies. A sad letter came from a lady in Tenby who was trying to sell her semi-detached house on the sea front, and an estate agent in Carmarthen sent us a foolscap sheet of information on a cottage that consisted entirely of two rooms and a large broom cupboard. We did not follow up either of these opportunities (although the Carmarthen estate agent almost had us believing that the broom cupboard was something worth looking at) but the other two replies were definitely of interest. They were both from farmers in North Wales, and the properties for sale were only a few miles apart.

It was September, and we had a week's holiday due to us, so we hired a van, packed up the camping kit, and drove up to North Wales.

We went first of all to Mr. P. of Bethesda. We found that he lived in a very large, modern, bungalow, and it was here we made our first encounter with Welsh hospitality and the Welsh way of doing business. There was no question of our going immediately to see the place Mr. P. was selling. First of all we had to have tea. We were taken into a large bay-windowed front room, which was obviously kept for 'occasions' and where tea was waiting for us. The three-piece suite, the trinket-covered piano, the trolley and cake stand—all seemed to date from the 1930s. There were several 'nests' of occasional tables bearing mats and pots. Everything was polished and cared for. Mrs. P., sixtyish, permed, powdered and well corseted, was proud of her front room and enjoyed giving tea to guests. But on this 'occasion' the guests felt a bit sheepish and out of place. We had come on a camping/cottage-hunt spree and were wearing corduroy shorts, old shirts and plimsolls. I balanced my tea plate upon my bare knee and tried to sip my tea in a ladylike manner, whilst we all exchanged polite small talk.

Mr. P. was anxious for us to appreciate that although he was primarily a sheep farmer, his interests were much broader. He had travelled, he told us. He was a deacon of the chapel and a member of the parish council. He was also chairman of the local Countryside Protection Society and served on the education committee. 'I've made a few enemies,' he said with a wink, 'but I've made a lot of friends too.'

It was apparent to us that Mr. P. had also made a lot of money. When we had finished tea he said that he would lead us up to Bryn Bras—the farmhouse that he was selling—and from the large garage of three cars he chose the Jaguar.

The lane up to Bryn Bras was a series of hairpin zigzags, each of which necessitated a three-point turn. The first mile was thickly wooded, but then the track emerged upon a high rounded hill, with the farmhouse squarely in the middle.

We didn't like it. It seemed solidly built, spacious and certainly worth the £1,950 that Mr. P. was asking, but we were intimidated by it. It was too high; it had a large cellar half-full of water, and it was too bleak. We could never cope with Bryn Bras. We crept away from it apologetically, feeling, somewhat guiltily, that we had eaten Mrs. P.'s cakes and sandwiches under false pretences.

The next day we drove across to see the other place that was for sale. It was Hafod. Our cottage-hunting spree was over.

When we got out of our van and glanced around at the view of rolling hills, valleys and mountains, it seemed that we were on top of the world. It was a golden September afternoon and there was a great silence around us. Our voices were shrill intrusions.

The rooms in the cottage were smaller than we had hoped for, but there was a neat cosiness about the place. There were two rooms upstairs and three down. The kitchen was quarry tiled and the stairway curved down into it. In total ground-floor space it was about half the size of our town flat. But there was a good range of outbuildings; a shippen, a stable with hay-loft, and two adjoining outhouses, one of which was obviously a chicken house. All were built of stone and all had good slate roofs except the chicken house which had a corrugated-iron roof. There was also a large corrugated-iron hay barn.

There were no mains services to the cottage. The water supply was a spring about thirty yards from the back door.

As we walked up the hillside to see the extent of the field

being sold with the cottage I began to feel very uneasy. It was some minutes before I could identify the reason for my unease. It was an attack of cold feet. Here was a cottage that seemed to be almost exactly what we wanted. I could think of no sound reason for turning the place down. I found myself sneakily hoping that the asking price would be too high. Self-doubt entirely occupied my mind as we walked up through the gorse. Was I a fraud? Did I really want us to spend all our savings upon a country cottage—or would I prefer to go on gaily cottage-hunting indefinitely?

The farmer selling Hafod would not put a price upon the cottage. He said that he was open to offers. He gave us permission to camp in the field that night whilst we thought it over, and he went away leaving the key with us. We looked over the cottage again; taking it all in this time. Wandering from room to room without the owner treading upon our heels, we were able to get the 'feel' of the place. Later in the evening, squatting in the doorway of the tent, we talked it over. Alan didn't have my tail-between-the-legs misgivings. His doubts were of an entirely practical nature—was he likely to get employment in the area—could we grow fruit and vegetables at this elevation 1,000 feet above sea-level in mountainous country—and what was a reasonable offer to make for the place? But he agreed with me that the finding of what appeared to be a suitable cottage did not fill him with elation. The fun was over. This was serious.

The next morning was misty, with a smell of autumn in the air. I walked on bare feet across to the spring to fill the kettle. The short turf was soaked in dew and delicious between my toes. Little clusters of wild pansies turned dew-decked faces upwards. Fancy owning a field that contains pansies and gorse and bracken! The little grey stone cottage looked sad and lonely huddled against the hillside. It seemed to be waiting. A pair of ravens in close formation flew strongly overhead. They *kronked* to each other in muted companionable voices. Somewhere out on the moorland a curlew was calling. I began to feel better about the whole idea. This would be a good place to live.

We drove across to see the farmer (who has since become

a very good friend of ours) and offered him £1,650 for Hafod. Our offer was accepted with beams and handshakes. The deal was clinched over a magnificent afternoon tea in the kitchen; and it seemed a thoroughly satisfactory way of doing business.

Before leaving North Wales, Alan went to the Employment Exchange in Llanrwst to enquire about work in the area. I sat outside on a wooden seat near the river to wait for him. Indian balsam was in full bloom along the river banks, and the warm air was heavy with its sweet musky fragrance. Sand-martins zipped to and fro across the river. Alan came out looking cheerful. 'There's not much work around here, but they reckon I should get fixed up with something eventually.'

Unfortunately the affable official whom Alan saw on this occasion was not there when he returned to report for work some twelve months later, and he had an entirely different reception.

2. TROUBLES

Hafod is an odd little cottage. It comprises two square stone 'boxes', one slightly smaller than, and adjoining, the other. The two boxes are in alignment at the front, so the larger one sticks out three feet beyond the other at the back. Each square box has one room up and one room down, and each has its own roof. The walls are about two and a half feet thick. A stone lean-to built onto the back of the larger side was the original dairy, and stone outhouses adjoin the cottage at either end. Having such an assortment of small, independent slate roofs has several advantages. It means that repair work is quite simple as only one small roof need be dealt with at one time; also we are comforted by the thought that if one of them should collapse in a storm we can at least hope to cower safely beneath another.

We have never considered it to be a particularly attractive cottage. When we bought Hafod it had a defeated, neglected air that still hung around even after we had moved in. On bleak, mist-wrapped days during November of our first year the atmosphere of gloom about the place matched my own feelings of homesickness at the time. We both gained a strong impression that no one had ever been happy at Hafod. This may well have been so. We learned from the deeds that the original holding was of twenty-three acres, so at this altitude, with its poor starved fields, it must always have been a sub-sistence farm. It would have been hard, frustrating work to try to gain a living out of this stony land.

Hafod was once part of a large estate that had owned vast tracts of land in North Wales since the days of Henry VIII. Its power began to crumble in the early part of this century, but the final break up and sale of most of the farms and small-holdings didn't happen until the 1950s. Hafod was probably always occupied by disgruntled tenants who were only waiting for an opportunity to get out into something better. They must have known hardship, poverty and possibly starvation. Certainly no one has ever loved the place. I wonder how many generations of despondent women have gazed from the kitchen window over the bleak moorland scene, thinking enviously of their sisters enjoying a softer climate and easier living in the valley? Those broken quarry tiles in front of the kitchen fireplace—were they the result of wood being chopped by some uncaring person, either too idle or too ill to do the job outside? Those savage hatchet marks in the parlour door —a frustrated teenager? Or a family row? Those piles of household rubbish within throwing distance of the front and back doors—could *nobody* be bothered to bury the stuff?

The people who lived in the cottage immediately before us were a young couple from London. Although we never met them we learned a little about them from our neighbours. The couple had a baby and had moved out to the Welsh countryside in search of a better way of life. They didn't find what they were looking for at Hafod. Within ten months they were back in London. The husband, we heard, was a jovial, cheery chap who had a job that he thoroughly enjoyed in the aluminium works at Dolgarrog. His wife, whose temperament is unrecorded, doesn't appear to have had anything to enjoy. Certainly there was no evidence of any attempt to make life at all cheerful for her at Hafod. All doors and windows were ill-fitting, letting in draughts and driving rain; the path to the spring was rutted and miry, and access to the privy was hampered by coils of barbed-wire designed to keep out the cattle and sheep. The old black range in the kitchen had been replaced by a combination grate that Cheerful Charlie had put in himself. But as no outlet had been made for the oven flues, the oven was useless—a joke which no doubt kept the happy man chuckling for months. His wife bought herself a Calor gas stove and moved out to the dairy-cum-back-kitchen where all the cooking was done from then onwards. The door to the

26

back-kitchen faces north west, and a gap under it gave access to mice, wind, rain and snow. I often imagined my predecessor standing at her Calor gas stove, with hailstones bouncing around her ankles in the north-west draught, peering mournfully into a saucepan by the light of a paraffin lamp—and wondering why she ever left London. No wonder the place had such a melancholy atmosphere.

One of the first jobs we did at Hafod was to take hammer, chisel and crow-bar to the useless combination grate in the kitchen and arrange for a modern solid fuel heat retention cooker to be installed. The demolition work was done on a week-end visit before we moved into the cottage, and we made arrangements for a local ironmonger to supply and install the new cooker. We had decided that it was essential to have a permanent source of heat in the cottage (how right we were!) and we also wanted two ovens, and a side tank to heat water. Our stove must be able to burn any sort of solid fuel (we had rights of turbary upon the moor which we intended claiming) and we wanted to be able to open the firebox door in order to enjoy the delight of an open fire burning in the kitchen. We bought the only cooker then available that fulfilled all these requirements—the Wellstood, Series G.N.

The stove was built into the old fireplace in the kitchen on the gable end wall, and as every other room in the cottage opens off the kitchen, 'Stove' is our version of a central heating system.

The two bedrooms open onto a tiny landing and the stairs curve down 'open-plan' fashion into the kitchen. A partitioned corner containing the sink and some shelves is the 'wash-up', and doors lead from the kitchen into the parlour and also the back-kitchen. The cottage is so small that someone standing at the stove can have a conversation with anyone else in any other part of the house without raising his voice provided the doors are open. The wall dividing the two parts of the house is 2 feet 6 inches thick, and little sound will pass through if the doors are shut.

So here we were in our country cottage. Our dream had been realized. But it didn't feel very dreamy. In fact, the dawning realization of the amount of work ahead made it more of a what-the-hell-have-we-let-ourselves-in-for nightmare. Prospective cottage buyers may, however, take heart. This is but a passing phase. You start by poking worried fingers at every flaking bit of paint and having heart seizures at the discovery of each woodworm hole ... but end up shrugging your shoulders at rotten joists and sagging roofs.

But when we found out about the water we hadn't got to the shrugging-off stage. In fact we hadn't moved in. We were the nervous new owners, just looking in for an odd week-end, and brightly reassuring each other that we had 'done the right thing'.

We had arrived with camping kit at the end of a week of very wet weather, and were a little bit put out by the obvious 1 foot high tide-mark around the parlour walls but decided, in our ignorance, that this was the result of damp rising from the earth beneath the floorboards, and that this sort of thing happened when cottages were left empty. But the tide came in again the next day. Then we *knew* that we had problems.

It was Alan who first noticed it. The evening was dark and wet, and we were about to leave for the drive back to Bristol. Bending to pick up his rucksack he noticed a trickle of water flowing over the step from the back-kitchen. He watched, fascinated, as this trickle of water curved around the wash-up partition and headed for the parlour door. Mystified, he opened the back-kitchen door and saw that half a dozen other trickles were assembling along the back wall and forming themselves into platoons of water that rolled purposefully across the floor towards the kitchen. At first we tried just mopping it up. But it was obviously gaining on us. So we tried sweeping it out of the front door. But it didn't *want* to go out of the front door. It wanted to go into the parlour. So Alan—never one to argue with wind or water—savaged the tongued and grooved floorboards at the entrance to the parlour and opened a 2 feet 6 inch hole giving onto the earth below. We arranged sacks on either side of the hole to discourage water from by-passing it, and the stream from the back-kitchen—now given a route that it was happy to take—dutifully emptied itself into the hole. When we left the cottage an hour later, water was still pouring in from the back-kitchen.

On our next week-end visit we tried to sort out where the trouble lay. We chatted about our problem to the neighbouring farmer, but he had no suggestions to make. So far as we could gather he had never heard of such a thing happening. The same puzzled incredulity was expressed by the man who kept the village shop two and a half miles away. There was much head-shaking, tut-tutting and bafflement. We were amazed. Did the couple from London wring out their sodden carpets and retreat to the City without saying a word to anyone about flooding? We could hardly believe this was the first time it had happened.

Behind the cottage the land rises steeply to a rocky spur at 1,110 feet. We call this spur The Bonk. The long wall of the lean-to back-kitchen was made of a motley collection of stones large and small, and we noticed they were all loose, unmortared and protruding at odd angles. It then occurred to us that the back-kitchen had originally been built into the sloping bank, and someone—comparatively recently—had been digging out a passage way between the back-kitchen and the sloping ground and they had left the unsupported back wall to fall about as it pleased. Moreover, they hadn't dug out low enough. The ground level in the excavated passage way was still about 18 inches above the level of the back-kitchen floor, and 27 inches above the level of the kitchen floor.

We were still not sure whether the flooding was caused by surface water rolling off the hill behind us, or springs right underneath the cottage itself. However, it seemed essential to get a system of drains around the back, so the following week-end visits were spent navvying. Alan worked with pickaxe and shovel and I carted the spoil away in a wheelbarrow. When we reckoned that we were low enough we laid a network of tile drains around the back and sides of the house. Then we got to work on the back-kitchen wall.

This was our first experience of working with stone and cement. Being completely unhampered by any knowledge of traditional building methods, Alan brought a fresh, un-cluttered line of thought to this and every subsequent problem. As this crumbling wall was supporting a slate roof the important thing was to stabilize and strengthen it with as little disturbance as possible. Cement was pushed into the wall with sticks, fingers and trowel, and the whole surface finally brought to a comparatively smooth and solid finish.

Inside the back-kitchen we laid a new 2-inch thick concrete floor on top of the old tiled one, and our final job was to saw 4 inches off the bottom of the wooden screen around the wash-up and fill in with a fillet of 'waterproofed' concrete. Sawing off the screen was a very awkward job as behind it is the 12 inch thick concrete floor of the wash-up. Alan had to sprawl full length upon the floor of the kitchen in order to accomplish it. From the bottom of the rotting screen we removed wedges of rag and newspaper—no doubt shoved there by a desperate previous occupant who was getting his feet wet. We hoped that our flood prevention methods were going to be more successful.

They were. We hadn't long to wait to see the effect of another heavy downpour. This time it occurred in daylight and we could see what was happening. After heavy rain had been falling for about twenty-four hours The Bonk was not only laced with torrents of ground water but was also sprouting several energetic springs. All this water was pouring down to the back of Hafod. We were delighted to see it being caught neatly by our drains. The outflow from the pipes on either side of the cottage was like water under pressure from a fireman's hose. Not a drop came into the house.

In the nine years that we have been here we have never since been troubled by water in the cottage ... but we are occasionally asked about it. The British Rail delivery man once asked us how we were coping with the water problem, and the postman also expressed curiosity. Shopkeepers in Llanrwst six miles away also knew about it. 'Let's see now; you live at Hafod. Isn't that where they have trouble with the water coming in?' Everyone knew about the flooding problem at Hafod except, apparently, our closest neighbours. From time to time, after heavy rain, we now get the odd casual enquiry from one of them: 'Much water in Hafod last night?' 'Water?' We shake our heads and look puzzled. 'Water?' We are baffled. We don't know what they are talking about. We can all play at that game.

The age of Hafod is a mystery. According to local legend the place was originally a squatter's holding. In the days before the Enclosures, when the common lands were shared amongst the common people, it was an accepted custom, we are told, for a man to stake a claim on a piece of land by erecting overnight a crude shelter. If smoke was coming from the chimney of his dwelling by the morning, then the plot of land on which it stood was his by ancient rights. The amount of land he could claim for a garden was decided by a personal feat of strength. Standing in turn at each corner of his dwelling, he flung a hatchet with all his strength. The points where the hatchet landed marked the limits of his territory.

The evidence of haphazard botchery about the place is quite in keeping with the suggestion that the original Hafod was thrown up overnight a few centuries ago. But it appears to have fallen down subsequently and to have been rebuilt a few times.

A slate floor discovered in the garden suggests a different layout of a previous house; an old doorway in a gable end has been filled in, and the walls of the larger side of the house have been extended upwards. Quantities of buried stone and slate suggest that another building has been demolished; and the roof timbers of the chicken house appear to be old ceiling joists from the parlour.

It seems to us that when Hafod was owned by The Estate, most building work—whether new or repair—was carried out with second-hand materials; and old fashioned methods were sometimes used with 'modern' materials. Trying to date our buildings by their materials and workmanship results, therefore, in total confusion. An adzed face of a purlin got us thinking romantically of the early eighteenth-century hands that wielded the adze—until we noticed the circular saw marks on the sides. We had a similar let-down with the oak pegged

31

hand-cleft slates on the shippen roof. When Alan went to replace a few—convinced that he was repairing an interesting old roof that had withstood at least three hundred years of storm and tempest—he was somewhat taken aback to find that the gaping hole exposed bandsawn rafters to which adhered the remains of machine-cut slates that had been fastened with galvanized wire nails. We have now been led up the garden path so many times that we are cynical of all discoveries and we place no significance whatsoever upon the fact that there are hand-made bricks in the kitchen chimney stack. The only date of which we can be reasonably sure is 1911 when the stable was built, and two other buildings were re-roofed. We owe this knowledge to 'J. Lloyd, Slater' who, in a desire for immortality, scratched his name and the year several times in the plaster torching.

To help us with repair work at Hafod we had bought a *Home Handyman Manual*, and we also made a point of reading books written by people who had repaired and converted old cottages. But Hafod didn't seem to be like other people's cottages. Other people's roofs were supported by interesting cruck timbers, or honest English oak purlins and trusses. The dodgy roof on the smaller side of Hafod is supported by purlins only—puny, soft-wood ones that have rotted at the ends. (Extra pieces of wood have been nailed to the rotten ends and these added bits protrude through the gable end walls. As they had never been protected from the weather, these too are disintegrating with rot.)

Other people, when repairing their cottages, apparently stripped off rotten plaster to reveal honest stonework that could be pointed up to become a wall of beauty. The rotten plaster we stripped off revealed slabs of crumbling slate, quantities of small random rubble and odd bits of worm-eaten wood. We hastily plastered it all up again.

Other people removed rusty old grates and found interesting open fireplaces behind, incorporating bread ovens, skillet hooks and massive oak lintels. The mean little modern tiled fireplace we removed from the parlour revealed a meaner Victorian one behind—with a dangerously cracked stone lintel to boot. Excavating behind this to uncover the 'original' one, we found ourselves peering into the chicken house.

Hafod, it seemed, wasn't the sort of cottage that people wrote books about.

3. MORE TROUBLES

Within a month of occupation it became obvious that a lot of the repair work was urgent. There was a top-to-bottom crack in the middle of the cottage front wall (at the junction where larger and smaller sides should have been keyed together, but weren't); the roof of the smaller side was obviously insecure; the back doors and jambs, and all window frames were completely rotten; and the place was damp. We consulted the *Home Handyman*.

'If your house is damp,' it said, 'check to see if gutters and downpipes are blocked or leaking.'

There *were* no gutters and downpipes.

In case this had any bearing on the problem we bought the only type of guttering and downpipe available locally—cheap grey plastic ones. Because of the wide eaves these were a great bother to fix and they rattled about noisily in the wind. During the next period of heavy rain we discovered that the *Home Handyman* obviously didn't know about Welsh rain. It doesn't fall down vertically from the skies, but comes driving along horizontally. It was battering straight at the walls, and up and over the roof—great gusts of it cresting off the roof ridge. The flapping plastic gutters were catching none of it. We eventually removed them and they are now cluttering up the shippen, along with a lot of other useless junk.

The *Home Handyman* was just as irrelevant with our roof problem. 'The weight of a roof,' it said, 'is shared between the purlins, the rafters and the wall plates.'

What wall plates?

There was a sliver of powdery cork-like substance visible between the top of the wall and the overhanging slates, but at the gable ends where the end-grain of the wall plates should have been visible, there was nothing. The main roof rafters (also powdery and corky) hung in the air. All the slates on this roof were loose. They rattled in the wind like chattering teeth, and several had slid off.

According to all the rules in the *Home Handyman*, this roof had no right still to be there. There was apparently no acceptable way of repairing such a roof. One could only pull it down and start again. But we couldn't afford a new roof. So we put away the *Home Handyman* and cautiously started work.

We 'insinuated' some bits of wood to act as wall plates at the gaping gable ends, and by discreet and cunning use of nails and cement secured them to the floating end rafters and the corky remains of the existing wall plate. The whole area of repair was then given a hopeful dose of wood preservative and coated with black bitumen paint. The slates, also suffering from old age and neglect, had originally been pinned to the roof battens with oak pegs. Pegs and battens were now disintegrating. The usual treatment for elderly slate roofs in these parts is to brush them over with a sand and cement slurry, but we didn't think that our purlins would stand the extra weight. As it was simply a problem of making sure the slates stayed in position, we decided to secure each slate to its neighbour with glazing tape. The tape was pressed firmly down, and smoothed and moulded with finger and thumb. Alan spent three weeks crawling over the roof before the job was completed. The neat lattice-work of tape effectively prevented any slates from slipping and we finally gave the roof two coats of black bitumen paint. Total cost of roof repairs —about £14; plus a blistered finger and thumb. Result? A first-class bit of botchery in the best Hafod tradition. The roof has given us no trouble since.

The crack in the front wall was worrying—especially when we stripped off the wallpaper in the parlour. The crack went right through. It varied in width from an inch to 3½ inches. We investigated further—removing rotten pebbledash rendering outside and loose lime plaster inside, and exposed a tall cavity. It seemed that a lot of the stonework had disappeared. We didn't stop to wonder how or why, but just got on with filling it up again. Stones and cement were fed into the crack and rammed down, rather like stuffing a chicken. Alan worked both from inside the house and out, standing first of all on the floor, then on a chair, then on a pair of steps, and finally on a ladder as the pillar of concrete grew inside the cavity. A final rough coat of cement and chippings outside and gypsum plaster inside finished the job.

The three windows (with double hung sashes) at the front of the cottage all needed renewing. The only type of re-placement window obtainable locally consisted of one large fixed pane of glass with a shallow top-hung glazed ventilator above. This suited us because we wanted to be able to look out at our view without peering between sash bars. We ordered the frames and glass, then, one by one on suitable days, we knocked out the old windows and put in the new.

The rotten back door on its hook-and-eye hinges was re-moved (the jambs came away with it) and Alan made a ledged door incorporating a fairly large sash. He hung it on a solid frame *inside* the opening which was later protected by a storm porch. Now no weather penetrates our back-kitchen.

The front door we considered to be worth saving as it was basically sound, solid and heavy. Only the lower 4 inches of the bottom rail were rotten and Alan sawed them off. He then faced the bottom panel of the door with a sheet of Vinyl flooring, topped with overlapped off-cuts of matchboard screwed in position and finished with a drip. We then built up the threshold to form a step to meet the new level of the door bottom. Finally we gave the door three coats of paint.

The front door and windows have continued to be a bit of a problem. They get such a pounding from the weather that no paint stays intact on them for twelve months. Moreover, if we have them fitting close enough to exclude draughts, then they jam solid when the wet weather sets in and swells the wood. Alan has now planed them off a bit, overlapped the gaps with beading, and settled for a compromise. Our doors and windows are no longer seized up from November to April, and when winter draughts become noticeable we simply put on more clothes.

It was only to be expected that the Hafod chimneys would belch smoke into the rooms. We had read that this was a common cottage trouble so we expected it—and got it. The kitchen chimney wasn't too bad and we have not felt obliged to do any repairs. When refuelling Stove she is inclined to belch a bit, and a sudden opening of a door can draw out a puff, but on the whole the kitchen chimney seems to work fairly well. The parlour chimney, on the other hand, didn't appear to work at all. Whether there was wind, or no wind and from whatever direction, the smoke from the parlour fire preferred to pour into the room rather than go up the chimney. It would work correctly only if the parlour door was closed, and the window wide open. We experimented with several mock-up canopies made of sheet steel and balanced in position upon stair-rods driven into either side of the throat, and we found that cutting down the fire opening vastly improved the draught. To be anything like trouble free, however, the fire opening had to be so narrow that it was barely possible to poke the fire without hitting the edge of the canopy, and only our feet enjoyed any warmth.

We tried various types of chimney cowls (static, rotatable and rotary ones) but none made any noticeable difference. Alan became convinced that the trouble lay largely at the fireplace and not at the chimney pots, and it was at this stage that we excavated the fireplace. When we knocked out the tiled surround we found that the work of filling-in behind had not been carried out and the large cavity there was undoubtedly a source of trouble.

Having made a strong repair of the wall where we had broken through to the chicken house, Alan rebuilt the fireback and sides with new firebricks, fireclay and high alumina cement; the general shape and size of the throat being decided by what he had learned from the canopy mock-up experiments. He introduced an iron bar beneath the cracked stone lintel, and filled in all holes in the flue up as far as he could reach. He incorporated an underfloor draught grate which takes air from ventilators in the front and back walls of the cottage.

The first fire lit in our newly built fireplace proved that

we had found the answer. It wasn't entirely satisfactory, however; little wisps of smoke still crept out every now and then from underneath the repaired lintel. So we brought back our adjustable canopy and stair-rods. By reducing the fire opening by just 3 inches the trouble was cured. The height of the fire opening from hearth to edge of canopy is now 16 inches and we can have magnificent roaring fires. Alan rescued the trivets from the combination grate that we had taken out of the kitchen fireplace, and built them into the hearth. The homely sight of a kettle singing on its trivet by the fire is now one of the delights of a winter evening.

With the smoking chimney cured, Alan turned his attention to other urgent matters, and the job of actually finishing the hearth surround was left. We still have our tinplate canopy filling up the necessary 3 inches of fire opening, and the plaster work around the fireplace is still waiting to be repaired. We have bought a large sheet of copper and, one of these days, Alan will make a 4 ft high copper canopy, and will build-up beside and around the fireplace with carefully chosen stones from the garden. In the meantime we sit before a temporary hearth of quarry tiles and a fireplace surrounded by honest repair work and expedient botchery. But it works—and that's all that matters.

Incidentally, the *Home Handyman*'s advice on smoking chimneys was limited to fixing a cowl or calling in a builder. But it did have one unusual suggestion to make: 'Perhaps you have troublesome wind currents in your location. Find out if your neighbours have trouble, and if so, how they tackle the problem.' What a good idea! We went at once to see what information we could gain. Our neighbours were sympathetic. Yes—they too had troublesome parlour flues. How did they get over the problem? Easy. They never used the parlour.

With the outside of the cottage looking patchy with various repair work, we decided that we would like to give it a protective and decorative coat of something or other. As both roofs were coated with black bitumen paint, we decided that an all-over wash of white would look the best. Starting with the front of the cottage (facing south-west) we scraped and brushed off all loose bits of pebble, mortar, lichen and moss, and gave it two coats of a much advertised cement-based masonry paint. Within three months it was washing off in streaks. We then tried an exterior-quality plastic emulsion paint. It lasted a year. On a north-west gable we tried a cheap oil-bound emulsion paint which has proved excellent. Now, seven years later, it is still in good condition. Unfortunately the manufacturers have since gone out of business—and we were never able to buy any more than the one gallon. We then tried a simple lime and tallow wash on all the other walls. Being unable to get lump lime we used bags of hydrated lime. To three-quarters of a 2-gallon bucket of lime we added about 1 lb of tallow, and mixed it together with hot water. We have found that this is by far the cheapest and most effective way of painting the cottage—albeit rather messy. You can't 'apply' limewash. You have to slap it on. So a protective dress of overalls, sou'wester and goggles is called for: a dollop of lime wash in the eye is no joke. On all but the front wall it has lasted very well. As no other covering lasted on the front of the cottage for more than twelve months we figure that we might as well use lime-wash as anything else. It's very cheap and lasts for a few years.

Our repair work on the stone outbuildings is crude, effective—and never ending. Sliding slates are fixed with glazing tape (if we have any) or cement. The stable is the best building of the entire holding. The massive truss supporting the roof is far superior to any timber in either roof of the cottage. The shippen appears to be much older. We are continually replacing slates, there is much repointing of stonework to do, and one of the roof timbers is badly affected by wet rot. The outhouse adjoining the south-east gable of the cottage appears to have been reroofed in 1911, but the new roof was never properly keyed into the gable. Sixty years of seeping rains have done their worst to the roof timbers and the end of the only purlin was a nasty mess of wet pulp and woodworm. Alan cut a stout oak post to a length equal to the height from floor to purlin, and notched the end to receive the angled edge of the purlin. He then wedged it into position, tapping the oak post at its base with a mallet until it was upright and taking the weight of the purlin. All done by eye and guesswork. A fillet of cement between roof and gable end wall has now stopped the rain coming in.

We have spent very little money on Hafod. Timber, glass, the under-floor draught fire, glazing tape, sheet copper and aluminium were all bought in the early days when things were not only cheaper, but also obtainable.

Living on a small and highly irregular income encourages a frugal outlook and heightens the skill of improvisation into something approaching an art. Nothing is wasted. Every jar, tin, length of wire, cardboard box, off-cut of wood or hardboard is carefully stored away against a possible future use. (When the door sills of the van rusted through, Alan patched them up with flattened-out cocoa tins, screwed into position and finished with cellulose fillers. When painted, the repair work was almost invisible.)

Our unorthodox patching up of Hafod has withstood the test of time, but our attitudes have changed. In the early days each fresh discovery of rot or woodworm filled us with gloom and alarm. Strange little creaks and taps in the night were interpreted as collapsing joists, shifting roofs or the death-watch beetle. Every repair job was tackled hesitantly, in case —in our ignorance—we should worsen the situation. But with the passing of a couple of years we gained confidence. We became bolder and more carefree. The first time that Alan went up on the main cottage roof he was nervous. He laid ladders up each side of the roof and lashed them together at the ridge. He then tied a long rope around his waist and lassoed the chimney stack with the other end. (That was a laugh for a start! He discovered some time later that the stack was so insecure, even the starlings gave it a wide berth.) The job was repointing the stack and then giving the roof a coat of bitumen paint, and for the first half day he crawled cautiously about the roof at the end of his rope in an awkward crab fashion. But by the end of the week he had lost his fears and was moving freely around the slates clad only in shorts and yachting shoes. Going up on the roof doesn't worry him now—which is just as well: he's up there at least twice a year in order to scrape out the kitchen chimney pot.

We now feel that so long as the walls remain standing and the roof stays on, then nothing else really matters. Whatever problem crops up, it is only a question of thinking about it long enough and a solution will be found. And between the two of us the job will be done. We no longer seek 'expert' assistance. We can't afford it now, for one thing, and moreover, as time goes on we are arrogantly convinced that, so far as the problems of Hafod are concerned, we know best. So it is a question of we do-it-ourselves, or it doesn't-get-done.

However, there is one trouble at Hafod that has beaten us. Condensation. From May until the end of October the cottage is dry and sweet smelling. This is the only time of the year we care to have anyone from civilized parts visit us. During the winter months most people would consider the place unfit for habitation. With the coming of the cold wet weather, the walls of the cottage in every room often stream with condensation. The kitchen and the parlour suffer less than the back kitchen and the bedrooms. Following shortly after the start of the condensation comes the mould. Mottled green patches appear round all window reveals and near the doors downstairs, and on the walls and ceilings upstairs. As winter progresses the green mould will turn to black and, if not removed will continue to thicken and sprout a downy fur. Any foodstuffs, clothing, shoes, etc., left touching an outside wall will become saturated and sprout beautiful little tufts of white fur, and every article in all rooms except the kitchen will be affected by damp. Clothing in cupboards or drawers, books and furniture, all become mildewy. Envelopes in the desk stick solidly together, and the books on the shelf go green and musty. (After a few winters here some shed their bindings.) Storage of dried food is a problem. There is nowhere in the cottage where we can guarantee that it *stays* dry. Packets of sugar and flour go solid. A 5-lb bag of tea stored in a bin once went green and swollen with mildew. We begrudged throwing it away and so tried a brew. It tasted perfectly satisfactory. We drank our way through all five mildewy pounds and suffered no ill effects.

Anything that needs protecting from cold or damp, or any article that we value, has to be stored in the kitchen during the winter. Field-glasses and cameras go in a drawer with the tea towels. The typewriter lives under the table with the sacks of potatoes. Bins and boxes of food are lined up against the the dividing wall. Herbs and onions hang from the ceiling. We came through last winter with a 1-cwt bag of cement on one side of the stove, and 5-gallon drum of bitumen paint on the other. Left in an outhouse they would have been ruined by damp and frost.

The bedroom over the parlour is uninhabitable in the winter. Condensation drips from the sloping ceiling onto the bed, and our breath condenses in clouds around our heads. So we move to the bedroom over the kitchen. Here it is necessary to have the bed in the middle of the room. We once slept with the headboard 4 inches away from the wall and discovered in January that the mattress was going mouldy beneath our heads.

When we bought Hafod the walls in each room were covered with a floral patterned wallpaper. We didn't like it and decided to remove it. The job was an easy one. The place was so damp that the wallpaper pulled off the wall in long lank strips. There were great cracks in the plaster through which the wind whistled, and there were also holes that let the mice in. We repaired all the plaster work and painted the walls with a primer/sealer. We decided not to cover again with paper because we wanted to know if any more cracks appeared. We gave the walls two coats of matt white plastic emulsion paint, and waited to see what happened. Condensation was what happened. We concluded that the walls were too cold to be left with a painted finish, so tried a different approach in the bedroom over the kitchen. Having scrubbed the walls with household bleach, and swilled them, we painted on an allegedly 'anti-mould' sealer as soon as they were dry. Carefully we covered them with expanded polystyrene sheets— using an emulsion-type adhesive which also was allegedly anti-mould. We then put on a heavy-quality anaglyptic wall-paper and finished it with two coats of a 'vinyl' paint to prevent damp air penetrating the paper. (We now feel that we should have used plain lining paper—but none was available locally, and it still isn't.) The ceiling was covered with ¼-inch 'heavy duty' expanded polystyrene sheet. The walls felt warm to the touch, and we felt sure that we had found the answer.

The following winter was mild and wet, and by December condensation was appearing in beads upon our new wallpaper. It also formed on the headboard of the bed and on chairs. The hooks on the back of the door dripped rustily and mould advanced from the window at its usual pace. Within five months much of the wallpaper had detached itself from the polystyrene, which was mottled with mould and soaking wet.

We have got around the problem in the kitchen (where only one wall and the wash-up are affected anyway) by covering the walls with flat oil paint then yacht varnish. This means that although the condensation streams down them, it is simply a case of mopping up the water from the quarry-tiled floor. And although a little mould appears it wipes off quite easily and leaves an undamaged surface behind. But we can't accept streaming walls in a room with floorboards and carpets. So the bedrooms remain a problem. Conditions in the parlour improved vastly after we had installed the under-floor draught fire (presumably because very little damp air enters the room). Only slight condensation appears on the walls and the mould is confined to a small area in the window reveals and a patch by the door. We have a fire burning in the grate every afternoon and evening on cold days and in this way we keep the contents of the room reasonably dry. If we leave the room unheated for more than twelve hours in winter, then the mustiness will creep back and any newspaper left lying there will be too damp to light the fire.

It was a comfort to discover that Hafod wasn't the only cottage in the area with such troubles. We got a sneaky satisfaction, when visiting our neighbours in the early spring, to note the spread of mould in the window reveals and the damp wallpaper bulging over the doorway. But our neighbours do not seem to be particularly concerned. Putting up fresh wallpaper every year is part of their normal routine. It is considered women's work, and it is always done in May, a few weeks before shearing time. This is the first occasion in the year when a farm kitchen will be filled with visiting neighbours who have come to help with the communal job of shearing, and every Welsh farmer's wife likes her kitchen to look good for the occasion. The fact that it will all have to be done again the following year doesn't seem to bother them.

We thought that we might get a useful exchange of ideas with the few English people who own holiday cottages in the village, but none of them will admit to having troubles. 'Oh there was a spot of damp when I bought it,' we were told, 'but I cured it with "Blanks's" anti-condensation paint,' said one; ' "X's" water-repellent fungicidal compound fixed it,' said another.

As we have tried (and failed with) all products made by 'Blank' and 'X' we would like to discuss it further, but we get no encouragement. We see continuous activity in and around the holiday cottages each spring: plaster being stripped off; new floors being laid; central heating systems being changed; new paint being applied ... but none of the English cottagers confesses to having problems. They've paid good money for these cottages and they're not admitting failure to anyone!

But there's no such reticence on the part of the occupiers of the two council houses in the village. Having no axe to grind they complain loudly of the damp. 'The walls do go black in the winter, isn't it!' one woman grumbled in sympathy with me. As the council houses were built of brick in the 1950s and, presumably, have cavity walls and damp courses, we can only conclude that condensation troubles are likely to be suffered by all inhabitants of houses on high altitude moorland—whatever the age or condition of the building—but we are surprised that we had not heard or read of such troubles before. The writers of our 'we-did-up-a-cottage' books refer frequently to 'rising damp' (whatever that is) which they soon set to and cured by all sorts of ingenious modern technological methods, or with the aid of 'Blank' and 'X'. Why don't any of them fail? Is it because, having written their books, they quickly move out before those telltale marks reappear on the walls? Mind you, we don't know why they are being so fussy. It's not 'rising damp' that concerns us, but the 'damp' that pours in torrents off the hillside behind us, or comes driving through the walls and under the doors in the teeth of a south-west gale, or appears out of the moisture-laden air to pour in streams down the walls.

Yet, in spite of living in conditions that would sometimes appal those with more refined sensibilities, we have both remained perfectly fit and healthy. In all the years we have been here we have had no respiratory ailments whatsoever—not even the slightest sniffle of a cold; neither have we suffered from any form of rheumatic disorder.

Sometimes the conditions depress us. Often, in the winter, we endure several continuous weeks of rain, when thick grey clouds hide the mountains and nothing is visible from the window except swirling mist and wet foliage; when it's so dark in the cottage we need the light on all day, and the mud from outside is brought in on our boots and cakes the mat and spreads around the floor. Then we sometimes look at each other and wonder what the hell we are doing here.

But all that's forgotten during the enchanting summer months, when doors and windows are open from dawn to dusk and the cottage is fragrant with the scents from the may blossom in the hedge or the elder blossom on the tree by the back door, and the garden is delirious with birdsong.

During severe winter weather the cottage has a dramatic appeal.

One January, when there came a lull in the snow that had been falling steadily for two days, I decided that I would like to walk to Llanrwst to do some minor and unimportant shopping. The sun was shining weakly from a pale blue sky, and the landscape was a dazzle of white as I crunched happily along our track. But three hours later, when I was on the way back from Llanrwst with a laden rucksack, conditions had changed. Snow was falling heavily as I passed through the village, and things had worsened considerably as I started up our track. The first half mile between the walls

45

was slow going. The road was rapidly filling in, and sometimes I had to scramble on to the wall to by-pass a drift several feet deep. But when I got to the highest part of the track where the walls have fallen, I realized that I could be in real trouble. A full blizzard was now blowing and fine snow was driving straight into my face. I could not see the track. Odd boulders and bent hawthorns came into view, but as I stumbled along I had no definite way of telling if I was still on the track or not. Suddenly a black shape loomed out of the snow in front of me. Alan had come to meet me. I grabbed him joyfully. 'Come on, it's bloody terrible back there,' he shouted. 'Let's hope we can follow my boot marks.' What a hope! They were distinguishable for about a hundred yards, and then they were obliterated and there was nothing to guide us. Nothing lay ahead but a vast white lumpy wilderness and a wall of driving snow. It would be possible actually to pass the gate of Hafod by a few yards and not see it. A few feet strayed in the wrong direction could take us off at an angle to perish somewhere in the uninhabited wilderness of the moor. Alan had thoughtfully brought with him some coffee in a thermos, some oatcakes and—with a pessimistic caution typical of him—the tent and sleeping bags. But there was absolutely no shelter here from the savage force of the snow, so that opening up the rucksack to get out the thermos flask was out of the question. We were now on the most exposed part of the track and for a few minutes we had to stand still because there was a complete 'white-out'. Although I was wearing a close-fitting hood, the snow was hurtling at my face with such stinging force that I could not look up at all. Alan was luckier. He was wearing an ex-Army parka jacket, with a large fur-lined hood that had a wired extension over the face, so that he could peer ahead through a protective tunnel. I got behind him, clutched his rucksack and kept my head down. We staggered along like a pantomime horse. I hoped that his sense of direction was better than mine; I had absolutely no idea where we were.

'There it is.'

I peered ahead, but could see nothing.

'Down there!'

We had climbed too far up the slope, and were about to pass Hafod. It lay below us on our left. I could just make out the collection of little roofs huddling beneath a thick cover of snow. We scrambled, fell and tottered down to the cottage. Against the front door there was a 3-foot drift, half of which came into the kitchen with us as we lurched in. A wave of warmth from Stove greeted us, and the delicious smell of a casserole from the bottom oven. Layers of snow slid off us and scattered over the floor. I beamed around at my cosy, homely kitchen and we exchanged jubilant expressions of relief.

'Good old Stove!'

'Lovely smell!'

'Christ, what a blizzard!'

Outside the storm could do its worst now. We had provisions in the house enough to withstand a twelve weeks' siege. We were safe.

4. 'MOD. CONS.'

The Water Board and the Electricity Authority don't bring their services to Hafod. No one has ever asked them to. The local council haven't tried to include us in any of their sewerage schemes—but this doesn't mean they have forgotten about us altogether. They write to us regularly each April, asking for payment of rates. As the only service of theirs that we use is the Mobile Library we think they are doing very well out of us. When Hafod was revalued for rating purposes we found we were paying rates as high as the cottages in the village—where all mains services are laid on. We queried this and received a long letter from the local Valuation Officer from which we gathered that rating assessments were based on the presumed annual rental value of the property, and as no one these days would dream of renting a property that hadn't been 'modernized', the landlord would obviously have to lay on mains services, and the fact that we hadn't didn't count! To quote from the Valuation Officer's letter: 'The lack of services does not affect the gross rental value as it is assumed that the landlord would have to provide the services to maintain the hypothetical rental.' Against such Alice-in-Wonderland logic there can be no argument.

We find it no hardship to live outside of The System. It has never been our intention to be connected up with any of the Public Utilities, so our energies have been concentrated upon making life comfortable for ourselves at Hafod without them. We haven't got a 'thing' about this. When we visit friends and relatives in town we are quite happy to pull their flushes, soak in their baths and use their electricity. It's just that we don't consider these things to be important; whereas

48

solitude, freedom and fresh air are. What's more, in some ways our system is cheaper.

Take Stove for example. Stove is the 'soul' of Hafod—radiating warmth and life, non-stop summer and winter. We let out Stove's fire once or twice a year for the purpose of maintenance and chimney sweeping, and the cottage feels dead until Stove is burning, crackling and belching smoke once again. The cottage never gets too hot, because in summer all doors and windows are open most of the day anyway. Stove works efficiently on the cheapest of coal, wood or turf and can even tick-over for a few hours on rubbish and stones. Sometimes, when we are down to the dustiest rubbish and the weather is damp and windless, Stove will be sluggish and unco-operative, but normally by using the draught controls we can decide whether we want Stove roaring hot, or just moderately warm. We are amazed at Stove's efficiency. A scuttleful of fuel a day heats a 22-inch-long hot plate, two ovens and a 16-gallon tank full of water. The kitchen is always warm, and we have gone all winter with no other source of heat in the cottage. (This was before we had sorted out the troubles with the parlour flue.)

Stove's overall length is 4-feet, and it stands 3 feet 1 inch from the floor. Things are put on it, hung over it and leaned against it to keep warm and dry. Backache can be relieved by squatting against Stove, and the best place for a pair of cold feet is in the bottom oven.

Stove hasn't always been trouble-free. We bought it through a local firm and asked them to install it. This was in the early days—when we went about things in the 'correct' way and got the 'experts' to do jobs for us.

Getting Stove into Hafod was a very awkward business. Our experts were certainly adept at lugging heavy bits of cast iron over rough ground, although they were somewhat casual with the smaller parts—tossing them around haphazardly. 'We'll soon have this fixed up for you,' said one Goliath, stepping backwards onto an oven door. I couldn't reply. I wondered how long the thermometer would stand his weight. They were a cheerful enough bunch, and didn't understand our anxieties. 'Plenty of stoves like this we've put in, isn't it,' the foreman assured us as he laid out the drawings carefully upon the window-sill. I might have felt happier if he'd put them the right way up, but as I doubt if he could read English anyway, perhaps it didn't make any difference.

We helped them to assemble the larger pieces but, by and large, left them to it. They borrowed Alan's tools, cadged nuts and bolts, and heaved the stove into place, breaking the hearth tiles that we had been hoping to preserve. Some small parts appeared to be missing, so were done without. We interfered only to insist that the hot plate was level (a whim they granted us) and decided to shrug our shoulders at the soot-box door that was set on the skew, and the elbow flue pipe that didn't line up with the smoke-box—thus causing a ridge that has been a hindrance to cleaning ever since. We breathed a sigh of relief when they went, and thought that our troubles were now over and that, on the whole, it could have been worse. It was. A year later the kitchen chimney went on fire.

As the chimney had been swept regularly, we were dumbfounded when it caught alight. We could hear the flames roaring away in the chimney breast just above Stove—and guessed what had happened. Twenty-eight hours later, when the panic was over and everything had cooled down a bit, Alan took hammer and chisel and broke through the tiles (now cracked with heat) and one course of bricks—and exposed a cavity with a little soot still glowing in the bottom. It was obvious that this large cavity had been gradually filling with tarry soot; soot which couldn't be got at, and which we hadn't known existed anyway. As there was now no way of filling in completely to ensure that this couldn't happen again, Alan made this point of access a permanent feature.

When the single vertical course of crumbling bricks was removed, the cavity measured about 4 feet by 2 feet and tapered up into the flue proper over a height of 5 feet or so. A foot below the access hole the infilling was loose and powdery, but this wouldn't matter as it would be covered by the new work. We put about 8 cwt of stones, bricks and Alan's 'patent' fireproof cement mix into the cavity and began to understand how and why our 'experts' had managed to install Stove so quickly. A 9-inch square soot-door was fitted in the new access hole which Alan then shaped to take a shovel nicely.

From the (now) two soot-doors the filling slopes up at 60° to meet the chimney flue which is about 2½ feet by 2 feet at this point. Between the soot-doors is a sharp ridge 18 inches high so that soot falls either to one or the other door and is cleared out once a fortnight.

Then there was the side tank.

Stove had been alight for only a few weeks when we noticed dark brown trickles of water oozing from the joints of the outside iron casing. Moreover, the water in the tank was turning yellow. Rust? Impossible. The tank was made of tinned copper. We'd insisted upon this as our spring water is very acid. We did nothing for a few days, hoping that the trouble would eventually 'go away' (they do sometimes) but the trickles were getting thicker and nastier, and the water in the tank was now a murky brown. Something had to be done. We let out the fire, emptied the tank and unscrewed the iron cover. And there lay our trouble. The underside of this cover was bare iron—now thick with rust. What's more, when screwed down there was a ¼-inch gap between the top of the copper tank and the iron cover, so that hot rusty water condensing on the cover could flow across this gap and find its way down through the casing of Stove. The trouble was soon cured. We dismantled the tank, covered the bare iron with zinc paint, reassembled the whole thing to a better fit, and filled the gaps with silicone rubber solution. Now, after nine years, the rubber is beginning to decompose on the surface, but the seal is unbroken and there are no signs of rust in the water.

Sometime later Alan happened to meet the manufacturer's representative in a local shop, and he mentioned this trouble. The man shook his head in amazement. 'No one's ever complained of that before.' Just our bad luck it seemed. A short while after this Alan was working in a nearby holiday cottage where he had been asked to fit some electric points. There was a Wellstood like ours in the kitchen, so he was naturally curious. Lifting the lid of the water tank he peered inside. It was full of rusty water.

We don't depend exclusively upon Stove for cooking. (Prudent, isolated moorland dwellers always have alternative courses of action up their sleeves.) We also have three Primus paraffin pressure stoves, and two camping stoves—one of which works on petrol and the other on methylated spirits. We can also cook upon the parlour fire. The same caution is applied to our lighting systems. We can provide ourselves with light from candles, or various lamps fuelled by paraffin or acetylene, but our main source of light is the wind, harnessed by 'Charlie' our windcharger. As Charlie is an important part of our lives here he deserves a chapter (the next) to himself.

Another important part of our lives is Minnie the spring. (So called after Minnehaha—Laughing Water. But the name is appropriate for less romantic reasons. She becomes 'Mini' in summer when she very nearly dries up, and uncouth friends are liable to burst out laughing: 'That's never your only water supply! Good God! Ha, ha, ha, ha! ...')

We have a great affection for our spring. Her mood changes with the weather. After prolonged periods of torrential rain she gushes in wild fury and you are liable to have the bucket dashed out of your hand. A long dry spell will reduce her to a feeble trickle. She has never actually dried up (although she has seemed pretty near to it on occasions) nor has she ever frozen. It usually takes about a fortnight for a change in the weather to produce any effect upon the spring, so its source must be well below the surface. The water seems to maintain an even temperature of around 45°F—which means that in summer it seems to be icy cold, whereas in the grip of a winter's night the springhead is wreathed in vapour. We dedicated the spring to Naiad—the goddess who presides over rivers and springs—but also took the mundane precaution of having the water analysed. It is crystal clear and sweet to drink and the Analyst, although not so enthusiastic as we are, pronounced it 'safe and suitable for drinking and domestic purposes'. We hope that Naiad wasn't offended.

Compared with the national 'average' figures, we use very little water. On most days the tank alongside Stove takes about a bucket and a half to top it up (3 gallons) and the cold-water storage tank about four buckets. Water for drinking is kept in the carrying buckets. They are white, so it is easy to see if any bits of dirt have dropped in, and they have close fitting lids. On washing days and bath nights we need to bring in an additional six or so buckets.

This may sound like a lot of tramping around with buckets. It is. But sometimes—when the spring is a real gusher—the job can be done in about ten minutes. But there are other times—when the water is reduced to a trickle so feeble that it is only a rapid series of drips—when the job could take all day. But you don't just stand there waiting for it; you leave the bucket there and collect it occasionally when you happen to be passing that way. Of course, if you *want* to take your time over fetching the water there are plenty of interesting things to look at as you dilly-dally your way along the spring path. You can see if there are any nuts forming on the hazel trees that we planted hopefully a few years ago; you can hang over the gate of the vegetable garden to see how it's coming along; how are the spruce trees doing? What about a look at the rhubarb? There is the spring stream itself, and the lower pool. There are tadpoles to be inspected, and frogs to be looked out for. Oh yes, there are plenty of things to dilly-dally over if you are so inclined.

But what about the times when dilly-dallying is not what you have in mind? Like when there's a couple of feet of snow obliterating everything, and more on the way; or when there's a sleet-laden south-westerly gale pushing you off your feet and spitefully lashing out at your wet hands? Then the whole performance becomes an expedition, a trial of strength: you against the elements and may the best one win. The result is usually a draw. *You* manage to get water to the cottage, but the wind scores points by (a) chilling your hands until they ache, (b) blowing you daft and (c) ensuring that at least a quarter of the contents of each bucket ends up inside your wellington boots before you make the back door. You collapse by Stove; exhausted but triumphant. Perhaps this explains why we don't use much water.

We bath and wash our hair on Sunday evenings. It's a matey occasion, in the kitchen, in front of Stove ... the one in the galvanized tub being douched with warm water and handed dry towels by the other. The radio is usually playing, and a pot of coffee brewing. We can recommend this as an ideal way of taking a bath ... provided that you don't get many unexpected visitors.

Bath night is followed by washday—and this seems to be everyone else's system here too. From my washing line in the garden I can see two other farms, way across the moor. And no matter how early I start upon my wash on a Monday, there will be a line-full of clothes billowing from each of my neighbours' lines before I start pegging out the first shirt. Do they get up in the middle of the night to start work? Or am I too slow? Certainly my washing seems to take up rather a lot of time.

First of all I have to sort it into piles—things that can be mangled; things that can't; woollies; and things that are to be boiled. I hadn't used a mangle before I came to Hafod— not a proper one (all cast iron with massive wooden rollers, huge hand-screws and great oily cogs) and I was surprised to find how efficient it was. Almost as good as a spin dryer. So I became a mangle enthusiast. All garments with zips, hooks, buttons or other mangle-impeding attachments were scrutinized calculatingly and, if possible, relieved of them. Pyjama jackets for a start. Who wants buttons in bed? I cut them off and sewed up the jacket fronts, leaving enough room for them to be pulled over the head. Alan's workshirts got the same treatment, also a few of my blouses. Brassières can be suitably adapted for feeding to the mangle, also summer skirts, but not trousers. Trousers have to be wrung out by hand, inch by inch, and sometimes they take days to dry. I haven't yet worked out a way of persuading Alan to have his flies sewn up.

My boiler is an old gas copper, adapted to work over a ½-gallon Primus stove. This is another time-consuming procedure. The boiler is half-filled with hot water taken by the jugful from Stove's tank. The Primus jet is pricked, the cup filled with meths and set alight, and the pressure release valve tightened. Whilst waiting for the stove to prime I will invariably go and do something else. And I will invariably forget all about it and come back when the meths has burnt out and I have to start all over again. Needless to say, I don't boil the clothes every week.

I take the washing to the spring for the final rinse and, as the boiler is in the back-kitchen and the mangle is in its own little outhouse, this means that I spend a fair amount of time trudging from place to place carrying bowls of washing. But on fine blowy days it seems worth all the trouble. My line stretches between the willow and the wych-elm and there is something intensely satisfying in the sight of it full of washing blowing in the sunshine. The sheets thump, billow and thwack; pillow-slips bulge, tea towels flutter crazily and the shirts reach out demented skinny arms to the bracken-covered hillsides. I end the day with a laundry basket full of clean dry washing, scented with sunshine and moorland air.

But it's not always like that. There are miserable, drizzle-shrouded days when the washing hangs sullen and limp, and comes in wetter than it went out; there are bitter east-wind winter days when, with fingers red and stiff, I can't prise the stuff off the line—it's frozen there solid: towels like sheets of hardboard, shirts that stand up by themselves. And there are bad-tempered days when the Primus under the boiler runs out of paraffin, the spring unaccountably spews out a load of dirt into my bowl of washing, and when the sheet that I have just eased through the mangle slips from my fingers and falls to the floor.

I once decided that washing on wet days was a dead loss and it would be far better to wait for fine weather. I chucked the dirty clothes into the spare bedroom, and took clean clothes from the cupboard as we needed them. But the time came when there was nothing clean left in the cupboard, and a mountain of dirty clothes in the spare bedroom. So I gave up that idea. Washing is done each week now, whether wet or dry and—if necessary—hangs dripping from the clothes-horse in the kitchen. This is where Stove comes to the rescue. A clothes-horse full of wet washing will dry overnight when placed in front of it.

I enjoy ironing. It is a soothing contemplative sort of pastime. It is also a highly suitable secondary occupation whilst listening to a radio play. It took only a few soot-blackened pillow-slips to teach me that it is advisable to wipe sad-irons on something else before thumping them from the hot plate to the linen. Having learned this I have nothing but praise for them. In fact, I cannot see how women were ever conned into abandoning them for the gimmicky contraptions trailing electric wire. There is nothing to go wrong with sad-irons. You can use them for propping up books, cracking nuts, holding open doors ... and they will still press your linen for you. You can heat them on cookers powered by electricity, gas, oil or solid fuel, or you can shove them in the fire. Having, in my maturity, discovered the sad-iron I am now immune from the blandishments of Hoover or Morphy Richards. Where I go, my sad-irons go. Friends and relatives no longer have difficulties over my Christmas present. They give me crocheted pot-holders.

I also have a paraffin flat-iron. This unlikely sounding appliance looks, in fact, rather like a modern steam-iron. Alan bought it for me to use on those occasions in high summer when the kitchen might be otherwise rather hot if I were to roar Stove in order to heat my sad-irons. I have never really been happy with it. Granted it works efficiently enough, but I am never at ease smoothing my sheets with this shining contraption with its menacing hiss. It's those occasional pops and spurts of flame out of the side that I find so unnerving. Whenever possible I find excuses to use my sad-irons.

People who know that we live without mains services express their horror mainly on two points. They don't mention washing day (which to my mind is the aspect most deserving of apprehension) but carry on about electricity and sanitation. The feeling of dependence upon electricity I can understand, but the affection for the flush toilet I cannot.

Thirty yards from the house at the end of a daffodil- and lily-lined path is a little stone and slate-roofed structure which, for the want of a better word I will call the privy. What *can* you call it? Up here it is referred to as the *Ty bach* (coyly) or the *Ty cachi* (rudely) and people who call ask for the 'toilet', the 'lavatory', the 'W.C.' or the 'penny house', none of which it is. Earth closet? It is not. Chemical closet?

We don't use any chemicals. It is simply a little stone house containing a wooden seat with a hole in it and bucket underneath. So I shall call it the privy.

People who live in communities where privies are the general rule don't make jokes about them. This is not because they are ashamed of them, or embarrassed, but because they are a part of life that is taken for granted and nothing particularly funny can be seen about them. But buckets that become filled have to be emptied—and sometimes one becomes a little dilatory about this chore. 'It's about time this bucket was emptied,' one will mumble to oneself whilst cautiously adding to its contents. But a few days may pass before one actually gets around to it. We all know that this can happen, so one never places a neighbour in an embarrassing position by asking to use his privy. When visiting, one 'goes' before leaving home. (Or, in this sort of country, one can 'go' whilst on the way if taken short.) But visitors from the city don't appreciate these niceties. And sometimes in the summer, when I hear a car door slam, and look out to see tidily clad people picking their way carefully up the path, I suffer a moment's panic. I never worry about the fact that I might have nothing to offer visitors to eat, but the thought that the bucket may be full sets me gibbering with embarrassment. If I can send them away quickly without giving them anything to drink I do so.

Mine is not an uncommon embarrassment. I worked for a while with another woman in a gift shop near Llanrwst. The privy there was a ramshackle wooden construction containing a rather unstable plastic bucket with a seat. No one ever actually sat upon the thing and as you were in complete darkness once the door was closed, it was all rather a case of hit or miss, mostly miss. The manageress of the shop was so ashamed of our privy that she forbade us absolutely ever to allow any customer to use it. She feared that the 'image' of the shop might suffer. As this is an area frequently filled with tourists, and the nearest public lavatories are in Llanrwst, urgent requests to use our 'powder room' were quite common. It seemed so callous to give someone a point-blank refusal, that we got around the situation by looking meaningfully at the woods surrounding the shop, and claiming that we didn't have any toilets on the premises. They invariably backed hastily away wearing expressions ranging from astonishment to disbelief. I don't know what it did for the 'image' of the shop—but at least it got over the refusal business in a more friendly manner.

The privy at Hafod is a solidly built little house of pleasing proportions. And the view is splendid. In fact I think that we could claim to own the privy with the finest view in Great Britain. Who else can sit at their daily duty whilst contemplating regal slopes of Moel Siabod, the soaring heights of Glyder Fawr and the great wide slopes of the Carneddau? No need for reading matter in our privy.

In accordance with our waste-not-want-not philosophy, the contents of our privy are deposited on the current compost heap, along with soot from Stove, wood ashes, vegetable peelings, grass cuttings, bracken and occasional dustings of lime. We take a year to build a compost heap—then we leave it standing for three years before opening it up. Squeamish readers will be pleased to learn that our three-year-old compost consists of a wholesome, peaty, fibrous mixture in which nothing of the original matter is recognizable.

Previous occupants of Hafod weren't so particular about emptying the bucket. They opened the door of the privy and tipped it out. Long-past generations of tippers might have left a fertile bit of ground behind them—if it wasn't for the tin cans, broken glass and coal ashes that they tipped along with the privy bucket.

Most villages round here now have some sort of sewerage, but get a few miles away from them and outside privies become the rule rather than the exception. (The visit of the night-soil cart is still a fact of life for many isolated hamlets.) The drains of civilization are, however, extending gradually outwards each year, and there are plans for laying on sewers to many places at present remote from any such system. Not everyone welcomes them whole-heartedly. I worked for a time for the engineers surveying locally in connection with a proposed sewerage scheme. Every householder had to be visited and asked which room he intended converting into a bathroom so that the pipe line could be worked out. One dignified old gentleman received us with typical Welsh courtesy and listened politely to what we said. 'And now Mr. Evans,' my colleague finished, 'perhaps you'll show us which room in the house you intend to use for your lavatory.' A look of horror crossed Mr. Evans's features. 'In the house!?' he said, his voice rising indignantly, 'we'll have none of your dirty English habits here! It will be in the proper place man. At the bottom of the garden!'

5. CHARLIE THE WINDCHARGER

If the provision of light for the cottage was left to me, there would certainly be no windcharger. I'm not too sure about paraffin lamps either. Especially the wickless pressure types. All in all we should probably end up with candles. Let it not be thought that I am complaining. Far from it. I am delighted that in our remote moorland hovel we can have light in all corners and can listen to civilized sounds from our radio and record playing equipment.

If you came into the kitchen and heard the bounding staccato notes of Rameau's *La Poule,* you could be forgiven for thinking that we had George Malcolm in the parlour, and the glorious noise of Holst's Planet Suite thundering out threatens the very fabric of the cottage and sends the mice scurrying for earplugs.

But these aesthetic pleasures are ours only when there is electricity. And when your energy source is the wind—unpredictable, merciless and moody—nothing can be taken for granted.

Since the winter when the miners' 'work to rule' and the Arab oil troubles introduced us to the era of the 'Energy Crisis', there has been a surge of interest in 'ecological housing' with 'low environmental impact'. Harnessing the wind to provide electricity has been suggested as one answer to everyone's problems. Do-it-yourself with your own little windmill on the roof. Why on earth hadn't we thought of it before? I'll tell you why. Having lived with 'low-impact technology' for nine years I am in a strong position to comment. The only person in a stronger position is, perhaps, Alan. And he's biased. He claims it's fun.

Let me start by exploding the myth that electricity from the wind is cheap. The cheapest way to light your house is by electricity produced by the Central Electricity Generating Board. The fact that *your* bills are so high is your own fault. You aren't content with just *lighting* your house. You want electric stoves, fires, deep freezes, flat-irons and the like. And *that's* what costs all the money. Compare your cost per unit of electricity with ours, and I shall prove to you that we are paying through the nose for our 'free-as-the-wind' electricity.

When we first came to Hafod we lit the cottage by candle and paraffin lamp. (This was cheap enough at the time—1965—but with the price of paraffin soaring this is now likely to overtake the windcharger in cost per unit of light.) So I will digress for a moment to talk of oil lamps.

To someone several generations removed from the daily routine of wick trimming and chimney polishing, the business of coping with paraffin lighting can be somewhat daunting. But with practice, patience, and the placid acceptance of half-lit gloom, you can come to be philosophical about the performance, if not actually to enjoy it. There are three basic types of paraffin lamp. The wick and mantle type which looks beautiful on the dinner table, but smokes evilly as soon as your back is turned; the wickless pressure mantle type, which has a matey hiss, is more robust and less draught conscious but liable to explode if over pumped; and there is the plain old-fashioned wick lamp. The last type is easy to light, behaves itself and is perfectly satisfactory so long as you don't actually want to *see* anything by it. The light from a plain wick lamp is just about sufficient for you to see to grope your way from one room to the next (opening the door slowly, or it will blow out in the draught) so it is handy to carry up to bed with you. But a candle does just as well ... and smells nicer.

However, our wide selection of lamps (which includes four acetylene ones) all maintained in trim working order, means that we can be sure of having some form of lighting, whatever happens to Charlie. And quite a lot happens to Charlie.

Why do we call our windcharger Charlie? Well, when the propeller is spinning freely in a stiff breeze it makes a very impressive swishing sound that will increase to a sort of whining, chuffing roar very much like the noise made by the blades of a helicopter. So we called him Charlie Chopper.

He was Alan's idea of course. After we had bought Hafod, but before we moved in, Alan set about the task of acquiring a wind-powered generator. This was not because the thought of living at Hafod without electricity appalled him, but because the thought of producing it fascinated him. Electricity has, apparently, always fascinated him. If I am to believe his mother, he abandoned his rattle in favour of cable and plugs at the age of eighteen months, was experimenting with flash-lights and bells at the age of six years, and built his own 2-valve radio set at the age of nine. At thirteen he was special-izing in building miniature radio sets in cigar boxes; had a telephone system fixed up with the boy across the road, and had the front gate wired up to ring a warning bell when any-one opened it. I understand that by the age of fourteen he had graduated to making bombs, but this was only a temporary anti-social phase and he soon returned to his first love, elec-tricity, and he has remained constant in his affection ever since. Nowadays in the course of a day's work, he is prepared to tackle almost any mechanical job and, to a lesser extent, carpentry and joinery. But if he can find an excuse to add a flashing light, or a ringing bell, then he is a happy man.

So, before we left Bristol, we advertised for a Lucas 'Free-lite' Wind Generator. Lucas's have not made these sets for twenty years, and it is not easy to obtain second-hand ones in good condition. We were lucky. Having heard that wind-chargers were still being used in the Scilly Isles, we wrote to the local council there asking if they knew of any that might be for sale. They did. The official who opened our letter wanted to sell his. What's more, he delivered it to our flat in Bristol. (We paid him £25. In 1954 it had been bought for £156 2s 0d with two 160 amp. hours lead acid batteries.)

It looked a very workmanlike collection of bits and pieces—propeller, tail vane, dynamo, two iron castings and various odds and ends—and I thought that as soon as we moved into Hafod, the whole lot would be thrown together one afternoon and that I could then switch on. But it was not as simple as that. First of all Alan had to overhaul it, then we had to buy a

stout oak post, some hefty wire stays, four 3-foot lengths of
3-inch by $\frac{3}{8}$-inch angle-iron (to drive into the ground as 'pegs'
for the stays), cable adjusters, various odds and ends and
several hundred yards of heavy electric cable. We also had to
decide upon the best site, and the house had to be wired up.
All in all it was six months before the lights were switched on
at Hafod. It was then that I began to learn something about
the snags of home-made electricity.

To begin with it was 24-volts, which meant that our previous
appliances were useless, and all our bulbs would have to be
ordered in bulk from the one remaining supplier who lived on
the other side of Great Britain. The radio and record player
could be easily adapted to operate on 24 volts d.c. (they had
been chosen with this possible conversion in mind) but electric
stoves and fires were completely out. By means of a rotary
converter* the voltage could be bumped up to 230 volts (or
240 volts) a.c. for occasional rare luxuries like the slide pro-
jector or the photographic enlarger, but the suggestion that it
might also cope with luxuries like the vacuum cleaner and spin
dryer was dismissed as this would punish the batteries too
much, and what was wrong with a stiff brush and a mangle
anyway?

Charlie was sited about a hundred yards from the cottage
at the top of our sloping field, amongst the gorse and rocks.
The cable ran down the hill to be connected to four 6-volt
'Heavy Duty' tractor batteries in the outhouse. The house
lighting system was connected via the monitoring and control
panel in the back kitchen. (This was not as supplied by Lucas
but was, of course, Alan's Brainchild.)

That first summer we discovered the main snag of owning
a wind-powered generator—that it is surprising just how many
days there are when there is insufficient wind to make it work.
For the first fortnight there was no wind at all. Charlie spent
the time just idling away at the top of his post, whilst our
newly bought tractor batteries steadily went flat on us.

The first time we saw Charlie's blade whizzing freely in a
strong wind we watched in reverent awe. And then we became

* This (at £30) was the cheapest way of obtaining 240 volts a.c.
from Charlie.

63

used to him. We left him to his own devices at the top of the hill, just casting a casual glance at the ammeter and voltmeter on the wall in the back kitchen, taking it for granted that the batteries were now being kept nicely charged—Alan occasionally checking the specific gravity and level of the electrolyte.* Sometimes, when the wind was coming up to a full gale, we wondered if Charlie would be all right. With blade screaming and the tail vane lashing around frenziedly it did occur to us that he might be suffering up there in the teeth of the wind. But we were reassured by the maker's instruction card which insisted 'never furl the charger except during maintenance'. This equipment, we understood, was made to withstand Hebridean gales, South American typhoons and Australian tornadoes. But not, apparently, a North Wales hurricane. The dynamo burned out during the first storm of winter.

So it was back to paraffin lighting.

We sent the dynamo away for repair and a rather old and worn replacement was sent to us instead. We vowed that such an accident would never happen again and that Charlie would be given the care he deserved. He has been. No sick hen could have more consideration. When the needle of the ammeter starts to swing beyond 10 amps we look anxiously up the hill, watching for signs of trouble. We listen to the forecast carefully, and if gales are announced at night, Charlie is furled before we go to bed. Sometimes, inevitably, we are caught out and a mild zephyr of an evening deteriorates into something nasty at about two in the morning and someone has to leave a warm bed to crawl up through the gorse and rock to secure the furling lever. That someone is usually me. I find it impossible to lie contentedly in bed when the wind is hammering at the walls and rattling the windows if I know that Charlie isn't furled. Usually, all I can get from Alan is a sleepy 'it's only a Force 6. Shut up and go to sleep.' If I question his ability to make an accurate assessment of the wind strength whilst his head is stuck under the bedclothes, I get a mumbled suggestion to the effect that if *I* am worried, then *I* had better go and do

* The first sign of deterioration in a cell is a drop in the electrolyte level, the second sign is a drop in density (compared with other cells in the same battery).

something about it. So it's on with the pullovers and raincoat, shove pyjamas into wellington boots, find a flashlight and out into the night. Sometimes I enjoy the self-righteous I-told-you-so satisfaction of having done the right thing, when in the light of morning the havoc of last night's gale can be seen in and around the garden, but mostly Alan is right. The wind dies down, and I find that I made an unnecessary nocturnal expedition up the hill.

Charlie needs a lot of maintenance. Sitting up there, exposed to the weather from all directions, he takes quite a hammering. He is basically a simple and crude piece of mechanism—a 6-foot twin-bladed propeller is mounted on the armature shaft of a (normally) 36-volt dynamo whose output is (theoretically) prevented from exceeding 20 amps by means of an automatic furling device. The dynamo is clamped to a headstock which is mounted on a pivot, and a tail vane holds the propeller to the wind—the whole assembly being carried on a 13-foot post. Hailstone-laced storms knock hell out of the propeller, which needs frequent reshaping with a spokeshave, and repainting. All moving parts must be kept greased and the main headstock bearing drinks up oil by the cupful. The commutator frequently has to be cleaned with sandpaper, and carbon brushes occasionally have to be renewed. Sometimes on a winter's morning we see the charging circuit dials at zero when we can hear the wind roaring in the chimneys. After a moment's panic we find that Charlie's propeller is iced up and frozen solid. Alan has fitted a button on the control panel to cope with this, and usually two or three jabs at it will break the propeller free; if not, then we wait for the day to warm up a bit and try the button again.

However, our system does score on one minor point. Our 24-volt (nominally 25-volt) lamps give much more light per watt* than normal 240-volt ones and, despite being subjected to as much as 48 volts (on one occasion) and frequently to 32 volts (when we forget to change over batteries)—not one has burned out in nine years of use, although there is some loss of light due to blackening of bulbs.

* We have tried various wattage lamps up to 100 W and find that 40 W ones (singly or in combination) are the most satisfactory.

It has often been suggested (by well-meaning friends) that we should fit a voltage control unit. But voltage and current regulators, by their very natures, waste a considerable amount of otherwise useful power. Some types do not control voltage any better than a sound battery will, and several would *discharge* a battery* under certain wind conditions which often are experienced here.

Charlie's 'cut-out' is set to close at 5.0 volts above battery voltage, 2.0 amps charge, and to open at battery voltage, 0.5–1.0 amp *reverse* current. These figures could be improved only by having a much heavier cable between Charlie and the cut-out (which is in the house).

But the weakest aspect of the whole set-up is the battery. And none of the 'environmentalists' has come up with an answer to this one.

A battery whose only source of charge is the wind must be capable of withstanding short periods of heavy charge, followed by long periods of no charge whatsoever. Lead acid batteries do not like this sort of treatment and they soon deteriorate.

Our battery replacement costs over the past four and a half years work out at about £40 per year, and this is where the fallacy of free light from the wind lies. (Unintentional pun.) If, for the sake of argument, you assume that we want two hours of electricity per day in summer, and eight hours per day in winter, an 'average' day's electricity would be five hours. But for at least a quarter of the time we are unable to have electricity because the batteries are in too low a state to use because there has been no wind. This means that our five hours of (40 watts) lighting for, say, 270 days of the year, is costing us about £0.74 per unit!

*Voltage regulations: extracts from two manufacturers' specifications
(A) Cut-out closes at 0.7–1.3 volts above battery voltage
     Cut-out opens at 2.4–4.8 amps *reverse* current
     Control level 28–29 volts

(B) Cut-out closes at 27.5–28.0 volts
     Cut-out opens at 2.0 amps *reverse* current
     Control level 27–28 volts

In 1966 we approached a well-known firm of battery manufacturers and asked them to quote us for two suitable 160 amp hours capacity batteries. They did—£2,385 12s 10d.

Admittedly this included delivery and installation, and a life expectancy of twenty-one years was claimed, but we could not meet the cost nor the service conditions. These no doubt admirable accumulators were of a lead acid type and consisted of four massive batteries of single-cell glass units on racks. They would have filled our outhouse from floor to ceiling. To achieve the twenty-one years of service it was essential to discharge at a rate not exceeding 2 amps when a total of 320 amp hours (approx.) could be expected during a voltage drop from about 27–21.5 volts (or thereabouts). But, there was one solemn qualification which rules them out for ever. It was necessary that (when not in use) the batteries were kept on a constant 1–1.5 amps charge—preferably from the mains supply!

We approached other suppliers of batteries hoping to find something more suitable to us. We failed. No one has been able to tell us anything about 'chloride' batteries (about which Alans knows nothing, but he believes they were used for house-lighting from just after the First World War until recently).

We were given to understand that the modern alkaline (nickel/iron, nickel/cadmium, nickel/silver) types suffer from the drawbacks of the lead acid ones previously mentioned, in that the cost is high and even more sophisticated charging arrangements are necessary. Their only advantages are—light weight, small bulk and heavy discharge tolerance, e.g. 900 amps. But who wants 900 amps!

Our present set-up consists of four 6-volt 'Heavy Duty' tractor batteries costing £39 (three years ago), two 12-volt 'Extra Heavy Duty' lighting batteries costing £66 (eighteen months ago) and one 1.2-volt nickel cadmium (sealed) cell costing £9 4s 0d (four and a half years ago).

The nickel cadmium cell with a nominal capacity of 35 amp hours is used to run a clock of the solenoid-wound spring type. We cannot properly meet the charging requirements so the stopper is unsealed and it is frequently refreshed with distilled water. It is charged by being permanently in series with a 15-

watt table lamp. With a full charge, this arrangement gives us GMT (or BST according to season) for about thirty weeks of the year and then we have to rely entirely upon clockwork—or make a point of specially charging the cell by having our table lamp on when we do not need it. (For the cost of this cell I figure that we could have bought enough Mallory (dry) cells to give us the right time for about 150 years!)

The 12-volt batteries were said to have a capacity of 105 amp hours 'at the nine-hour rate'. But we didn't wish to discharge them in nine hours. We wanted them to last for three weeks from a fully charged state. When new they just managed to do this, provided we used only one 40-watt lamp (and nothing else) for three hours each day. After twenty-one days, unless at least a Force 5 wind sprang up from over the mountains, it was back to good old reliable Aladdin.

The capacities of all the batteries we have used dropped rapidly from new and at eighteen months with '105 amp hours' ones we are lucky if the lights don't fade on the sixth windless day. This works out at a capacity of 30 amp hours measured over a voltage drop from 27 at full charge down to 21.5 when—for practical purposes—they are fully discharged. By this time, of course, the other set of batteries (now three years old) is virtually useless and cannot be used for lighting at all.*

Having a full battery also presents problems. In the early days when we were operating with only one, we found that if we left Charlie running when the battery was fully charged then the voltage was pushed up to a height which set the lights flaring and brought nasty off-tune noises in protest from the radio. We were frequently furling Charlie just to have trouble-free radio listening. So we bought another battery and now have two circuits operating—one on charge and one in use. This meant having another set of controls and monitoring devices, and the panel in the back kitchen is now an impressive display of several d.c. and a.c. voltmeters, ammeters, change-over switches, test lamps and switches, relays, chokes,

* Batteries no longer able to provide us with lighting have proved satisfactory for automobile use.

condensers, resistors, fuses, spare lamps, spare fuses, tools and a very neat web of wires in various colours and sizes. (It also means that we have *two* batteries deteriorating and requiring to be charged.)

When there is a photographic session going on and the enlarger is in use, the rotary converter (ex-naval, continuous rating) must be brought into operation. As the converter going at full blast can devour the contents of a full battery in a couple of hours, it is obviously sensible to leave Charlie running in the hope that he can maintain the charge of the battery in use. Sometimes Charlie produced *more* than was being used and the consequent higher voltage over-ran the enlarger lamp—thus spoiling some prints. There are things on the market to cope with such problems but not only do these waste power, their acquisition would also deprive Alan of the satisfaction of producing an answer to the problem by his own gadgetry. So he produced a stepped variable resistor which consisted of a rotary 5-position switch from an early motor car, the wire element from an electric fire, part of a photographic flash gun body, part of an old typewriter ribbon mechanism, a small handle from an early hand fretsaw tensioning device, the shank from a broken Archimedean flat drill bit and various odd scraps of copper, brass, aluminium, screws, nuts, washers, bushes, etc. This enables him to use the oldest battery for enlarging—provided that Charlie is pushing out around 15-20 amps. The resistor controls the input to the converter and is adjusted with reference to a voltmeter across the loaded converter output.

A final thought upon batteries—and one for the 'environmentalists' to ponder upon. It has been suggested that if each one of us had our own wind-powered electricity generating plant, our overall national fuel consumption would be less. But, surely, the total energy used to provide suitable batteries for the plants would be greater than the batteries could ever return?

It is in the field of battery technology that more research must be done before we all get euphoric about electricity from the wind.

(All the technical confusement in this chapter was supplied by Alan—without whose assistance it would have been written in half the time.)

6. GADGETRY AND BOTCHERY

A damp, mouldering cottage with a crude electricity supply seems hardly the place you would expect to find photographic colour processing going on, nor would you expect high quality audio reproduction. The fact that both are part of the Hafod way of life is due entirely to Alan's persistence in the face of such recurring problems as oxidized switch contacts, damp-affected loudspeaker cones and corroded speech coils. As the quality of sound is the best that I have heard anywhere, *I* consider that our audio equipment must be very good. Alan dismisses it as 'typical modern crap' and is never satisfied with its performance. An evening spent listening to the record player or radio is a very restless affair for him. Whilst I sit back and listen happily to the music, he will be for ever hopping in and out of his chair to reposition a speaker or adjust balance, treble or bass controls, grumbling all the while of 'poor over-load characteristics' or 'rumble'. He announced his intention one day of buying a 'double-stacked 6-element array' (aerial to you) and I hoped that this might cut down some of his musical-chair activity whilst the radio was operating. Far from it. Not only does he still fiddle with the loudspeakers and knobs, he also complains of 'birdies' and 'twitter' then goes rushing out into the garden every now and then to adjust the aerial.

It seems to me that Alan is quite unable to appreciate any form of audio reproduction unless he is completely free to fiddle with it. His agony when politely listening to records in a friend's house is all too obvious. He sits there, grim and tense, with fingers just itching to get at the controls. Let our friend leave us alone for an instant and he will be across the

71

room and at the knobs almost before the door has closed. The equipment of one of our friends was far more expensive than ours, and although I do not hear mention of 'overload' and 'rumble', the talk is of 'excessive treble response', 'skating', 'flutter' and 'wow'. Why the hell they can't just sit back and enjoy the music I don't know!

Whatever the problem at Hafod, Alan will produce a gadget to overcome it, or a botch to get around it. Stove is festooned with hooks, handles and knobs to enable me to hang things, lift things and open things without getting burnt. I don't have to grope dangerously beneath my boiler to extinguish the Primus—it is accommodated upon a sliding tray, and provided with an extension pressure-release knob. But he also produces gadgets for where there are no problems. Like the complicated system of six pulleys, two bell cranks, four springs, three pulls and 12 yards of hemp line that enables you to put out the light from the wardrobe or the bed, when two paces could take you to the switch pull at the door. Then there is the subtle contraption that prevents the back door from opening. Other people find that a bolt is a suitable means of securing the back door. We have to have two bolts, plus an ingenious little cranked device that swings neatly into place over the latch arm and totally immobilizes it. This particular gadget is of great frustration to overnight guests. Especially those in an early morning hurry. Having undone the bolts they fumble frantically at the latch and cannot understand why the door won't open.

Having a gadget-minded husband might be a comfort—if only the gadgets stayed the same. But they don't. Alan, constantly seeking perfection, is always looking for ways to modify or 'improve'. Having got used to the idea that I make 'A' work by pressing 'B' and turning 'C', I find one day that it has all been changed and 'B' has to be screwed. 'C' has been abandoned and instead 'D' has to be lifted.

The lighting in the kitchen is a classic example. We used to have two lights fixed into the ceiling, and two switches on the wall. We now have two lights in the ceiling, plus one in the wall over the table. There are four switches on the walls, plus an illuminated pendant double switch, and a switch upstairs on the landing. The idea is that you can come in the front door and put on the light with one switch, and can put it off by the switch near the parlour door, or the one near the back-kitchen door, or the one upstairs. The light over the table is operated by its own wall switch, or the switch by the parlour, or the switch upstairs, or the double pendant switch, or the one by the front door—but not the switch by the back door. (Are you still with me?) The pendant switch operates the light in the wall over the table, or one of the main ones, and also its own little light. The object of this lighting system is, I am told, 'to achieve simplicity'.

Whilst Alan is around to turn off lights that I put on by mistake and to switch the radio through to the required loud-speakers (there are five pairs scattered around the house) then everything is all right. It's on the rare occasion when he goes away that I'm in trouble. Peeling the potatoes whilst sitting in a bedroom listening to a radio play has happened more than once. I never remember which way I have to turn which knob to transfer the sound to the kitchen speakers, and I'm terrified that the thing will blow up if I do something wrong. But the kitchen lights remain my biggest hurdle. Going to bed on my own one night I turned off the switch in the stairs and found that I had put on an additional light instead. I turned it off again and went down to switch off the remaining light, and was left in complete darkness to negotiate the length of the kitchen and the stairs. So I operated the pendant switch in order to get the tiny light, but put on the lamp over the table plus one main light. I thought that one of these might turn off with the other kitchen switch, but found that I was putting on a third light. I said to hell with this, threw the main switch, and went to bed with a candle.

When Alan came back after two days he found the battery flat, Charlie furled, the kitchen light switches turned on but the main one off ... and me reading by the light of an old wick lamp. He concluded that there are some fools against which *no* system can be made proof.

The botchery that has been carried on at Hafod is skilled, cunning and, in some cases, almost artistic. Perhaps I should define botchery. There is, after all, botchery and *botchery*.

Botchery is the tackling of a job by an 'unqualified' person using materials that he happens to have and unconventional methods. The person who spends money to do a job, or whose abilities are the result of any form of professional training, is not a genuine botcher.

There are two species of botcher. One is the humble botcher—a cheerful and optimistic character, with a hammer, nails and common sense. The other is the precision botcher. The precision botcher is a much more sensitive fellow. He owns hundreds and hundreds of little metal boxes containing an assortment of screws, nuts, bolts, nails, washers, springs, collars, clips, terminals, bushes, rings, hooks, rods, plates, plugs, knobs, discs, strips, straps, bars, etc. and dozens of cardboard boxes containing 'useful' parts from other people's abandoned appliances, quantities of unassorted pieces of wood, metal and plastics, and a wide selection of tools from clockmaker's broaches to grubbing mattocks and tack hammers to paviour's mauls. The two types of botcher specialize in completely different types of work. For example, let us take a hypothetical rabbit hutch, to be constructed (a) by my father or (b) by my husband.

My father is a good example of the humble botcher. If someone came to our house with a surprise gift of a pet rabbit, my father would wander out to his shed, pick up his hammer, find some nails, an old wooden box, some roofing felt and a piece of wire netting, and in about forty-five minutes he'd produce a perfectly satisfactory rabbit hutch. Whereas a pet rabbit presented to us at Hafod would cause great consternation. Alan is a precision botcher. He would cry out in alarm that he hadn't got any suitable wood, and that he didn't know anything about the requirements of rabbits. If he could be persuaded to have a go at the job, he would first of all get a book about rabbits from the library and, having satisfied himself with regard to required sizes of sleeping quarters, feeding troughs, mesh and gauge of wire netting, he would set about constructing a veritable rabbit mansion, and might get it finished in about five weeks. In the meantime, the rabbit would have been accommodated quite happily in a cardboard box which it probably preferred anyway.

On the other hand take, say, an ornate but broken Victorian musical box. Ask my father to repair it and he would shake his head sadly. Victorian musical boxes are beyond the scope of his hammer and nails—whereas Alan's eyes would gleam with delight. He would ferret out some 50 s.w.g. brass pins, tiny screws, slivers of various hardwoods, glue, shellac, gold-leaf and mother of pearl, and achieve a cunning repair that would delight the most critical of Victoriana experts.

Alan's botchery has kept the house and all our household things in repair and has also produced 'new' furniture. For example, when we felt the need for some form of small open-fronted cupboard to take an assortment of box files and flat folders, Alan produced one. It stands in the parlour and, on a casual examination, appears to be an attractive mahogany cupboard with a polished top decorated with a pattern of inlaid mother of pearl. It moves easily on concealed castors, and anyone who didn't know much about such things might date it as early twentieth century or late nineteenth century. It is in fact a large wooden packing case, cunningly faced, shelved, embellished, stained and polished ... and cost nothing.

But at Hafod we really need a humble botcher as well as a precision botcher. Although it can clearly be seen how a humble botcher could make a mess of a job that was really in the province of the precision botcher, it is not readily appreciated that the reverse is also true. Take the case of our letter-box.

The front gate at Hafod is a wooden five-bar one. It is a very old gate and (like everything else at Hafod) should have been scrapped long ago. It is frail, worm-eaten, and held together with netting and barbed-wire, but until we can afford to replace it, it will have to do. With the gate we inherited a letter-box. A simple construction with a flap lid, made of hardboard and wood nailed together—it was obviously the work of a humble botcher. Over the years this box has been gradually falling to bits and has on occasions been nearly torn from the gate in the wind. Each time Alan screwed it back on again he declared his intention of making a new box, but he didn't get around to doing the job until the day when a parcel of screws that the postman was delivering plunged straight through the bottom of the box and burst open upon the ground. I (being the true daughter of a humble botcher) could see no reason why another simple box of hardboard and wood nailed together couldn't be made to replace it. After all, the old one had lasted more than nine years before its final disintegration. But such reasoning is not in line with the precision botcher's methods. *His* box was *never* going to disintegrate. So he set to work. The box was made from 1-inch pitch pine, 1½-inch mahogany, double roofed and lined with laminated synthetic resin sheets. All joints were lapped with beading, and drips cunningly arranged to carry off storm water. The front entrance flap was faced with aluminium and weighed with cast iron. The back was constructed in four sections; two fixed, one removable for maintenance purposes and one piano-hinged (for extraction of mail) and fitted with catch, hasp, staple and padlock. A metal grid was placed inside for letters to sit upon, and provision made for drainage through a small pipe at one corner. The whole contraption was given five coats of paint. This box was going to stand up to a hundred years of weather. Any intending vandal would have to come equipped with dynamite, and its very weight would keep it from budging throughout the stormiest of hurricanes.

Reverently we carried the new box down to the front gate. The remains of the old box were removed, and the new one was bolted in its place. It was one of the strongest, heftiest bits of botchery that Alan had ever produced—in fact, a shade *too* hefty ... Three days later the gate collapsed.

7. GARDENING FOR FOOD

We wanted to grow fruit and vegetables. We also wanted to grow pansies and daffodils and hollyhocks and roses and wall-flowers and lots and lots of trees, but FOOD was the first consideration. We have always assumed (quite rightly) that our income would be precarious, but so long as we had a roof over our heads, a log of wood to burn on the fire, fruit hanging from a tree and a few rows of spuds—then we wouldn't actually starve or freeze. But it was the 'fruit hanging from a tree' bit that worried us. A glance at the map showed the 1,000-feet contour line passing just behind the cottage. Does fruit hang from trees at 1,000 feet above sea-level? We had a sneaking suspicion that it does not. What about other fruits? Root vegetables, greens and pulses? Would some of these also be denied to us because of the altitude? After we had agreed to buy Hafod, but before the official contract was drawn up, we decided to seek advice on the matter.

We had a fortnight's 'grace' in which to dither, so we sent off letters of enquiry to two of the Agricultural Seats of Learning (at Aberystwyth and Bristol). We described the position of Hafod, and the aspect of the land. We said that we thought the soil was the sort of thin, acid, moorland rubbish you would expect (or words to that effect) but that this didn't concern us unduly because we hoped, in time, to put right any deficiencies. It was the unalterable limits imposed by the altitude that bothered us. Just before the fortnight was up we heard from Aberystwyth. Without doing an analysis of the soil, they said, they were unable to help us.

Assuming that Great Agricultural Minds think alike, we decided not to wait to hear from Bristol. Which was just as well; it was six weeks before we received a note from them. They said that in view of the location they had forwarded our letter to their colleagues in Aberystwyth.

So, without the benefit of any expert advice, we set about making our decision.

There were blackberries growing in the hedge, and nettles at the back door. That was hopeful for a start. But it was the sight of 'the garden' that encouraged us most. 'The garden' was a rather self-conscious square at the side of the house that had been fenced off from the hillside. We identified it as a garden because there was a large wych-elm right in the middle of the plot, and it was the only place where there were any cultivated flowers growing; one clump of pyrenean lilies. (We later discovered two daffodils and a patch of snowdrops.) There were also two old tyres, a mound of rusting cans, some galvanized iron sheeting, a tangle of broken barbed wire and the remains of a motor-cycle sidecar ... but it was the grass that impressed us. Tall, green, strong and rich, it was the most luxurious patch of grass we had ever seen. Alan waded through it, up to his thighs in the stuff. 'Where this grows, anything will grow,' he said, with a knowing confidence born of total ignorance.

So the contract was signed and Hafod became ours.

We have since been able to identify that grass. The strains we are growing so well at Hafod are as follows:

Type of grass	Soil conditions indicated
Yorkshire Fog (*Holcus lanatus*)	Wetness and sourness
Bent (*Agrostis vulgaris*)	Poverty and unsuitability for root development

Add to this the fact that we also grow lovely clumps of rush, hawkbit and bird's-foot trefoil, and any passing agronomist could have told us that we might as well pack up our spades and return to the lowlands. To make a garden here was impossible. But we didn't know that. So we started digging.*

We were, admittedly, puzzled by the apparent lack of any sign of cultivation in 'the garden'. There was one small square patch where it seemed that someone had half-heartedly started to clear the ground—but that was all. We took the line of least resistance, finished clearing this patch, and planted our first seed potatoes there. They yielded about a pound of potatoes per haulm, which we thought wasn't bad. The following year we had a bed of kale there, but since then we haven't gardened in 'the garden'. Like everyone else, we have abandoned cultivation there. I don't really know why; the soil is no worse than anywhere else at Hafod, but the place just doesn't *feel* right as a garden. I hang out my washing there, and it's a useful place to cut and stack logs. The old tyres and motor-cycle sidecar are still lying around, but for most of the year we can't see them. They are completely hidden by that magnificent grass. We now refer to this area as 'the wych-elm plot'.

We created *our* garden in the field.

The field originally came right up to the cottage walls at the back and one side. A short bank topped with barbed wire prevented sheep from actually walking in through the back door, and a small gate in this fence led to the field and the spring. A neighbour's sheep and cattle normally grazed this field (an arrangement we were going to allow to continue for the time being) but we weren't too happy about the free-for-all at the spring. A drainpipe had been shoved into the hillside to give the water a lip to fall over, and around this pipe the cattle stood, slobbered, pranced and relieved themselves in muddy contentment. They *liked* standing in the spring

* We have learned to keep an open mind on the theory that plants can be used as 'soil indicators'. I can show you a patch of ground here where bird's-foot trefoil, clover, moss, sow-thistle, chickweed, groundsel, bracken, goosefoot, buttercup, foxglove, self-heal, rush, daisy, sheep's sorrel, yellow rocket and knapweed all grow together. According to our various reference books, this indicates that we have rich, very acid, gravelly, calcareous, well-drained, poor, wet, sterile, loamy, undrained, fertile, dry, sour, markedly alkaline, marshy clay soil.

water, and weren't too co-operative about getting out of the way when I advanced with my buckets. The water from the spring ran in a small stream down the field and formed a pool in front of the wall dividing the field from the track. We decided to fence off about a third of an acre of field, encompassing the spring and stream, but leaving the bottom pool for the livestock. This was to be our garden.

Have you the remotest idea what it's like to be standing in a third of an acre of starved, stony, sloping ground, with nothing but a spade in your hand and ideas in your head? We found our feelings ranging from positive enthusiasm at the start of the day, to Christ-what-have-I-taken-on despair at the end. Alan—who was the one with all the ideas—would tackle the job in a fury of inspiration, working from dawn to dusk excavating, earth shifting, banking, ditching, levelling. He would keep this up for about three days and then collapse in a heap, and refuse to lift anything heavier than a screwdriver for the next five. I adopted a more dogged approach. Working at the speed of an arthritic slug, I brought my horizons right down to the job I was doing. This bucket of stones must be collected from here and carried across and dumped there. Backwards and forwards, backwards and forwards, thinking about nothing, except stones and my bucket. I would allocate myself a set time for stone shifting, and then go and make a cup of tea. Tomorrow I might decide upon ground clearing. And for two, slow, mindless hours I would push in the fork, lever up a turf, turn it over; push in the fork, lever up a turf, and so on.

Gradually, between the two of us, we began to make an impression upon the hillside.

The first year we were appalled by the weather. Seedlings shrivelled up in the cold winds, and were then washed away in the floods. Peas and beans were smashed flat by the winds.

In the second year we battled with the weather—digging ditches around the vegetable plot; erecting wattle hurdles for protection, and planting a 'shelter belt' of a hundred 18-inch high Sitka spruce trees.

In the third year we were beaten by the weather. Our flood ditches filled up and spewed over; our hurdles fell to pieces with the constant battering of the wind; and our spruce trees were ripped from the ground and scattered around the hillside like so much litter.

In the fourth and fifth years, we started to come to terms with the weather.

A glance around at the landscape should have warned us what we were in for. Where rowan and hawthorn trees bend at permanent right angles, man wasn't meant to plant Jerusalem artichokes and rhubarb; where winds are so cold that privet loses its leaves every winter and elderflowers *never* turn into fruit—man was never meant to ripen marrows and onions. Not unless he's cunning. And breaks all the gardening rules.

And just to prove how good we are at breaking the rules, let me list the crops that we grew fairly successfully last year —our eighth—at Hafod: lettuces, radishes, beetroot, turnips, swedes, parsnips, carrots, Jerusalem artichokes, potatoes, peas, broad beans, kales,* broccolis (nine-star and purple), Brussels sprouts, onions, shallots, garlic, rhubarb, raspberries, blackberries, blackcurrants, gooseberries, redcurrants, strawberries, Japanese wineberries. We also have thriving beds of mint, chives, parsley, thyme, sage, marjoram, rosemary, and savory. We faced last winter with a harvest of 4 cwt potatoes, 27 lb of swedes, 32 lb of parsnips, 36 lb of carrots, 26 lb of Jerusalem artichokes, 16 lb of dried peas, 40 lb of onions, 15 lb of shallots, 6 lb of garlic and 5 ripe marrows.

My storecupboard was bulging with 30 bottles of raspberries, 10 bottles of blackberries, 12 bottles of gooseberries, 6 bottles of blackcurrants, 4 bottles of strawberries, 3 bottles of wineberries, about 24 lb of various jams, 3 lb of redcurrant jelly, 5 lb of rowanberry jelly, 10 bottles of beetroot, 12 jars of various chutneys and a large collection of dried herbs.

How's that for a harvest from a scrubby bit of barren moorland?

Apples, pears and plums we haven't tried. (Even our methods couldn't succeed with these.) And we haven't been successful with all vegetables either. For example, we've al-

* Scotch, purple, cottagers' and asparagus kales.

ways had complete failure with runner beans, cauliflowers and (strangely enough) leeks.

The reason why we are now successful where previously we failed is that we have learned to garden by instinct. Or, to be precise, Alan's instinct. In the unlikely event of me being asked where a certain thing should be planted, I would take into account aspect, shelter from the wind, and which was the easiest place to dig—and make a decision accordingly. Alan will put it somewhere because 'it feels right'. The strange thing is that, with Alan's planting, it will *look* right too. Have you ever heard of anyone transplanting turnips, swedes and parsley? Probably not. But Alan does it, quite successfully, each year.

We had started by consulting books. And that was one of our first mistakes. People don't write gardening books for places like Hafod.

The winters are long. Snow and sleet can be falling, off and on, from the beginning of November until the end of April. (We can still see snow on the eastern slopes of the Carneddau in June.) With our spring weather in May often being dry and cold, nothing really starts to grow here until June or July, so our season is very short. But what is most disconcerting of all is the havoc-wreaking ferocity of the wind, and the extremes of wet and dry conditions. Several weeks of dry weather can reduce the soil in our vegetable garden to a powdery dust with a hard cracked surface. Long dry periods are usually followed by long wet periods—and then we are in trouble. The floods at Hafod have to be seen to be believed. The moorland above us is like a vast peaty sponge that will happily soak up a few days of torrential rain. But when days of rain continue into weeks, then the moorland sponge reaches saturation point. The rain continues to fall, and the moorland streams tumble in a frenzy of savage brown water down to the Conwy Valley. But still the rain falls, and great pools of water sheet the boglands. The water-table will rise and then, suddenly one day, all hell is let loose upon the hillside above Hafod. From every crevice, molehill, mouse hole—or straight through the soil—sprout jets of water. Then a few more, and more. Before our eyes water will spurt from the ground in jets a foot high. The whole hillside becomes a flowing sheet of swirling water. You can guess what it does to the garden.

Our first efforts at trenching were inadequate and our seed bed was ruined. We now maintain trenches of about 18 inches to 2 feet around the vegetable plot. From here, and from other points around the garden, the flood water has to be led away to the track beneath the cottage. What happens to it then is someone else's worry. By culverting under paths, and digging channels that lie with the slope of the ground, we try to persuade the water that hurtles annually through the garden to follow the same route each time. And we try to make sure that nothing impedes it. Keeping all these channels and ditches clear is quite a job, a job which sometimes gets neglected. So when flood time arrives, all other work is dropped and it's outside with mattock and pick, clearing the flood routes of grass and earth.

The first crops lifted at Hafod were a poor starved lot and we decided that somehow we had to improve our poverty-stricken soil. We became frantic composters. Grass-cuttings, bracken, weeds, vegetable peelings, dust, soot, rags, wood ashes, paper, sawdust, the contents of The Bucket … anything that was compostable was added to the heap. Already known to the family as scroungers of old clothes to wear we now became scroungers of old mattresses. There's nothing like a good wodge of flock, straw, kapok or hair for mulching or composting. We built magnificent heaps up to shoulder height, and they rotted down in about three years to knee-high mounds of rich, wholesome compost. Now, at last, our plants had something to feed upon. Sometimes I will go out upon the hillside with buckets and gather up some sheep droppings but, on the whole, it is the compost that enriches our soil. Only once did we try a bag of chemical fertilizer—on half of the crops. There was no noticeable difference between the crops that were fed chemicals and those that weren't. (Having eaten at the house of a friend who uses nothing *but* chemical fertilizers, I will accept that they can make a difference. His crop of kale looked so much prettier than ours. It was the brightest of bright greens, whereas ours is always a dull dark green. We had some of his kale at dinner. It tasted like boiled cardboard.)

One of the sorriest sights I have seen at Hafod is the garden after a night of early autumn gales. Artichoke stalks lying at all angles; peas and beans a tangled mess on the ground; potato haulms snapped completely off. And our first efforts at planting shelter-belts of hedges and trees failed depressingly. We planted 18-inch Sitka spruce trees in blocks to the north-west and south-west of the vegetable garden. Following the instructions in our book on the care of trees, we removed all the grass from around each tree—and kept it removed. Allowing grass to touch the bottom branches of the trees was harmful it said. So what happened? Each tree, unable to get a footing in the loose shaly soil, wrenched backwards and forwards each time the wind blew, and carved for itself a round hole in which to joggle about. Came the first strong winds and these trees were simply torn out of the ground. Collecting the savaged trees from the hillside and stamping them back into the ground became one of our routine morning-after-the-gale activities. We gradually became fed up with our tree plantation, wrote it off as a dead loss and neglected it. The grass grew long and lush, completely covering the trees. When the winds roared across the moor, the long grass rippled in waves, and no trees were blown away. When we waded into the plantation in the autumn to see what was left, we were delighted to find our young spruce trees growing quite happily. So we didn't pull the grass out. We laid it flat around each tree and trampled it down. When the winter came this grass formed a heavy wet mat and effectively kept our spruce trees pinned to the ground. Thereafter we let Nature take over in the plantation—interfering only as the grass began to die back in the autumn, and we put away the book on tree planting. Our spruce trees need no help from us at all now. They stand—some of them over 12 feet high—an effective buffer to the winds.

We had similar difficulties with hedging. 'Hawthorn', said the book, 'will grow anywhere.' Admittedly, our nursery-bred plants didn't blow out of the ground, but they didn't seem to grow either. In fact they seemed to shrink. Each year there was less and less hawthorn to be seen, and then it quietly disappeared. Privet is another comparative failure. It is still with us, but mostly thin and stunted. It loses its leaves each winter and seems reluctant to get dressed in the spring. Now beech we were sure would be successful. We had seen thumping great hedges of it on Exmoor, making marvellous wind-breaks. We bought 100 beech plants (four years old, 12 inches high) and set them at the recommended 18-inch intervals. Four years later our beech 'hedge' consisted of 58 little plants, 12 inches high, standing 18 inches to 5 feet apart. Now, after having been growing for eight years (and with all gaps filled in) it is nearly 2 feet 6 inches high. However, we do have some excellent hedges in other parts of the garden— some of them 8 feet high and 2 feet thick. These are Alan's 'home-made' hedges, contrived from slips of laburnum, various wild roses, hazel, willow, sycamore and elder—each twiglet and branch being encouraged to weave around its neighbour for mutual support. Although quick-growing hedges like this need the support of a few strands of wire, this is a method of hedge making that we can recommend—even if the books don't.

You won't find many books recommending a weed-covered vegetable plot either. But we find it helps a lot. A covering of small weeds helps to hold powdery soil together and prevents erosion in the winds and leaching in the rains. It stops the soil from drying out completely during hot dry spells and, provided they don't get too tall, they are never likely to do any harm. We keep the seed bed weed free to allow the seedlings to get going, but once they are able to hold their own we let the weeds creep back again—interfering only if a crop is in danger of being smothered. But it is surprising just how much smothering a vegetable plot will stand. We once had to leave our garden for most of the summer, and the whole area was waist high in weeds when we returned. We were able to salvage a lot of the crops, but the biggest surprise was the onion bed. It was obvious, from the dense growth over all that not an onion had seen daylight for about three months. Yet from underneath all the weeds we lifted one of the finest, ripest crops of onions we have ever had.

Immediately surrounding the vegetable plot is a wilderness of trees, grass, docks, nettles and thistles where mice, voles, weasels, slugs, insects, frogs and toads carry on their affairs of killing and being killed, without interfering very much with us. (Snails are a rarity here. In nine years we have seen only three.) We get very little trouble with pests in the garden. Why, for example, should wire-worms attack our potato crop, when grass roots (their natural food) are in abundance all around? For the same reason we get no trouble from the birds. We have enjoyed the sight of bullfinches feeding greedily upon dock and sorrel seeds in late winter, and they were completely ignoring the newly budding fruit bushes nearby. Blackbirds occasionally pull out the seed peas and steal raspberries and currants—but they also pick the caterpillars off the Brussels sprouts and kale plants. Taken all round we are on the winning side.

This wild and prolific growth all around us not only protects our crops, but protects the creatures that attack the creatures that attack our crops—if you see what I mean. It also protects creatures that are useless—but beautiful.

Alongside the garden, and threatening to engulf it, is a large and ever growing patch of willow-herb. But we daren't remove it. For here feed the larvae of the large elephant hawk, a beautiful and fascinating pink moth that comes out with the dusk in June, surely one of our most handsome flying insects? Throughout the summer, peacocks, red admirals, small tortoiseshells and painted ladies dance through the garden. And where would they be without the nettles and thistles? If we want orange-tip butterflies and small coppers, then we must grow lady's smock. So we do.

Butterflies? Moths? I can't think of a single use for any of them. But how do you assess the value of enchantment in a garden?

8. GARDENING FOR FUN

Weeds that we feel obliged to remove from the vegetable plot are not necessarily composted. If they are interesting or pretty, they are transplanted. We do not differentiate between flowers that grow wild and flowers that are cultivated. Speedwell and pimpernel make a pretty carpet beneath the *Cotoneaster horizontalis*; dainty fumitory tumbles untidily beneath the moss rose; hawkbit and dandelion blaze a golden trail down the front drive, and there is a magnificent giant hogweed by the gate.

The front garden is a wedge-shaped piece of ground, hedged on two sides by hawthorn—the head of the wedge being made up of the cottage and the shippen. We made a heartening discovery in this garden. The consequence of many generations of mucking out the shippen was a goodly amount of ancient manure, in some cases a foot deep, over a wide area. There was also a goodly amount of broken bottles, tins, ashes, bones, docks, nettles and couch-grass but—once cleared—we had a very rich (albeit steeply sloping) patch of ground, sheltered on all sides. This became our fruit garden and here, in neat terraces, grow our blackcurrants, redcurrants, gooseberries and strawberries. (Raspberries, we find, grow better in a poor dry soil, so they are planted elsewhere on an 18 inch high bank.) The front garden is a bit of a sun-trap, so here we also grow our herbs. Mint, marjoram and savory are in clumps; rosemary, southernwood and lemon balm mingle at the base of a rose hedge, and one long bank is a fragrant array of lavender, sage, cotton lavender and variously scented thymes. Thyme and parsley line the paths, and the bees and butterflies go about their business all day long. On warm sunny days I will find any excuse to be in the front garden. All portable household tasks will be done there. I have peeled potatoes, mixed a cake, shelled peas, cleaned shoes, written letters and darned socks whilst sitting in the front garden. I have also sat there and done nothing.

The right places to sit in a garden have to be discovered. They cannot be decided in advance. Alan once erected a two-seat wooden bench beneath the laburnum tree because it was sheltered from the wind, caught the sun and looked out towards Moel Siabod. On a few occasions we took out our cups of tea and sat there selfconsciously, but it didn't feel right. We would find ourselves drifting across to a patch on the drive about ten feet away, and we would stand there to finish our tea. So we moved the bench there. It caught all the sun, but was not so sheltered and didn't have quite the same view —but it *felt* right. 'The lawn' is another non-sitting place. The 'lawn' is a flat patch of grass we have maintained outside the kitchen front window. In a hillocky, sloping garden, broken up with trees and bushes, it is handy to have a flat open piece of ground to do such jobs as cleaning carpets, disentangling pea netting, and taking a bicycle to pieces, but we have never wanted to sit there.

We sit mainly at the spring.

Question: How does a drainpipe outfall and a muddy pond in the middle of a field become transformed into a tranquil grotto in a copse where water splashes between rocks into a clear pool; where ferns jewelled with droplets grow in secret places, and where lizards lie upon sun-warmed stones between the flowers?

Answer: By hard work, love and magic.

The hard work came from Alan. In wellington boots, sometimes with a spade and mattock, but mostly with bare hands, he worked with earth, water, rocks and plants. The love came from both of us. Each stone was placed thoughtfully—bearing in mind the creatures that might like to live behind it or under it; each plant was placed where we felt it would be happiest.

The magic? Well, that came along afterwards, when we weren't looking. It's there now; but it's elusive stuff, magic.

The spring is now hidden from sight by the trees, and as you come to it around the curve in the path you feel that Something Magical has just slipped away, over there, between the spruce trees ... or downstream, between the mollyblobs and rushes. Only very very early on a summer's morning will you capture the magic at the spring. But then, on such a summer's morning the whole garden is filled with magic.

All paths, Alan insists, must be level. But they must not be straight. To make curved but level paths on sloping ground means a lot of digging out, banking up and step-making. Where paths are dug out, banks must be retained by walling. And walling is best held in place by sprawling cushions of saxifrage and stonecrop. Wandering around the garden is thus a peaceful meandering pastime, with pleasant surprises at every corner. With the possible exception of the front drive. Well, it's pleasant enough for us—but not necessarily for visitors. Especially those who come at night. Without torches. The front drive used to lie in a straight line from door to the gate. Straight lines are offensive to Alan. So he savaged the front drive—introducing beds of this and clumps of that— so that in order to make the front door from the gate it is now necessary to take one left turn, one right, one left, two right and one left. A hapless visitor, intent on Good Works for the Chapel, called on us one night with his collecting box. After staggering between some Lawson's cypresses he walked slap into the standard may tree, which must have given him quite a thump (it is supported by an iron stake), then found himself floundering about in the bed of gooseberry bushes. Two paces of solid drive must have convinced him he was at last on the path, until he went headlong over a small rockery, ending up on his knees in the Michaelmas daisies. It was here that he lost his box. Reduced now to crawling on all fours, he hit his head upon the garden seat. Feeling his way around the rhubarb bed and along the shippen wall he finally ended up on our doorstep in a state of great agitation, no doubt wondering what Godless barbarians found it necessary to live in such a place with a booby-trapped front drive. We had him in, gave him a cup of coffee, and eventually conducted him back down the drive by torchlight. We retrieved his box for him, and felt obliged to contribute a two-bob piece to show willing. (We hopefully searched the Michaelmas daisy bed the next day but made no 'findings'. The only thing our visitor left behind was a trail of damaged plants from the gate to the door.)

The cottage stands roughly in the middle of the two-thirds of an acre of land that now comprises our garden. This includes the bit fenced off from the field, with spring and stream; the front garden and the wych-elm plot. Within this area of land there were six trees when we arrived—two ash, one rowan, one elder, one willow and the wych-elm. There are now many hundreds. A veritable forest is growing up around us. We keep meaning to go out and count the number of trees, but we invariably get side-tracked and the job never gets completed. The hundred Sitka trees were the first ones we planted. Since then we have bought many other evergreens—Lawson's cypresses, noble firs, giant firs, red cedars and Scots pines—all planted with screening and shelter in mind. Fifty or so Japanese larch trees were added—quick growing, long-suffering trees that stand with bare branches all winter but cover themselves with a fluffy shawl of pale green needles in the spring. Then came the broad-leaved trees, in ones and twos. Ash saplings that took a couple of years to find their feet, but are now thrusting skywards with long straight fingers. Tiny-leaved rustling birch trees, handsome sturdy sycamores, various willows, hazel, elm, oak, alder, bird-cherry, blackthorn, beech, elder, hawthorn, laburnum, rowan and horse chestnut. Each tree had a personal struggle for survival during its first few years here. Some didn't make it. But the Hafod forest is now growing with such speed and virility that we are having to think about coppicing. Not every tree can be allowed to grow to full size; they are planted too close together.

We didn't have to *buy* all these trees. The laburnum was a gift, but most of the broad-leaved trees were saplings rescued from road 'improvement' schemes. (When we have seen bulldozers at work we have always tried to precede them. A clump of cowslips and a patch of blue pimpernel were saved in this way, also some dyer's greenweed, white and yellow melilot and one cornflower. The cornflower bloomed exquisitely for one summer but, alas, failed to seed itself.)

Trees are now beginning to appear at Hafod of their own accord. With nothing to interfere with them, seedlings of the ash trees, rowan, hawthorn and wych-elm are now sprouting up impudently all around the place. (If Welsh uplands were not grazed by sheep they would soon become natural forests once again.)

Letting things grow where they seem to want to is part of our way of life at Hafod. If a strong, healthy foxglove chooses to grow in the doorway of the outhouse, we will walk around it for two summers rather than disturb it. The giant hog-weed by the front gate is a bit inconvenient, but it obviously *likes* it there, so who are we to interfere? We always allow things to go to seed. This means that honesty and sweet rocket can often be seen blooming in the vegetable garden; poppies appear upon pathways, and kale plants grow in flower beds, fruit garden and wych-elm plot. We have often been glad of these self-set kale plants. Sometimes they are far better plants than the ones we have sown at the 'correct' time of year in the vegetable garden. Also the rabbits—for some obscure cussed reason known only to rabbits—have on occasions preferred to break through the fence surrounding the vegetable plot and devour our kale rather than eat the kale freely available to them in odd places around the garden.

Saving our own vegetable seed has so far proved entirely successful. Our kale, Brussels sprouts, nine-star and purple broccolis, spinach, beet, peas and beans are now grown wholly from home-saved seed. This year we hope to save seakale, beet, onion, parsnip and swede as well. We usually choose two good specimens of whatever food plant we wish to go to seed, being careful that no close relatives are allowed to flower nearby. On occasions in the past when we have been able to compare sowings of home-saved seed with 'fresh' shop seed, the home-saved seed was vastly superior—even when a few years old. Germination of home-saved seed is almost a hundred per cent and the seedlings are strong and healthy. Remembering some of the miserable, feeble shop seedlings we have grown in the past we now think that many of our previous failures were not altogether due to the foul weather conditions up here. I know that it is a legal requirement for the 'date of packaging' to be stamped on all seed packets—but this tells you nothing about the age of the seed inside that packet.

Parsley we don't need to save. It seeds itself quite happily all around the place and we can go out and pick parsley any time of the year except during prolonged severe weather. We also—against all the rules—successfully save our own 'seed' potatoes, and have done so now for eight years.

The muddlesome appearance of the garden, with its unkempt grass patches, tangles of hedgerow and confusion of weeds and crops, would not appeal to many people. In fact—taking into account the patched-up cottage and the evidence of much unfinished work around the place—it's perhaps not surprising that occasional passers-by think that the place is abandoned. 'Oh, we thought it was empty,' they say in embarrassment, when caught climbing over the gate or (on one occasion) trying the back door.

Although we have a set of documents that gives us legal title to these few acres, we do not consider that we own them. How can this land *belong* to us? We are just two of the animals that happen to be resident here for the time being. We are glad that, because of our efforts, more plants and animals are living here now than there were before, but this has only come about because we accepted that Nature (for want of a better word) is really in charge. We can't stop the wind blowing—we can only baffle it a bit by planting trees; we can't stop the water flooding—we can only divert it a little. We haven't created anything. We have only introduced the conditions in which things create themselves. Because we planted conifers, goldcrests and redpolls have come to join us; because we let the grass grow long, willow warblers and whinchats nest with us; because the ground is left undisturbed, trees can regenerate themselves; because we leave thistles to seed, goldfinches feed here; because we leave nettles to grow, peacock butterflies breed here; because we dam the stream and make a pool, tadpoles arrive; because we make a rockery with stones, lizards come to use it. Because we tend our garden with love, magic is here.

9. WILD CREATURES

It was a pity about Conservation Year. There were probably more animal, bird and plant habitats destroyed then than in any other recent year. All those committees of Earnest Ladies, intent on 'tidying the place up', and urging the local councils to remove 'eyesores'! We knew of one such eyesore. No doubt officially classed as 'derelict land', it consisted of about seven acres of scrub-covered quarry spoil, a deep quarry pool and a few ruined buildings. There was nothing offensive in its appearance. It was fenced off and all you could see from the road was a tangled mound of bramble and small trees. Impenetrable by fastidious tourists, and of no interest to local farmers, the place was one of the finest sanctuaries for flora and fauna that we have ever known. Tiny lichens, mosses, ferns and stonecrops grew in and around and over the ruined buildings, scrub birch, aspen, rowan, ash and least willow covered the slopes. Blackberries and whinberries grew in juicy profusion and everywhere was the scuttle, flutter and song of birds. Wren, robin, chaffinch, blackbird, blue tits, willow tits and long-tailed tits seemed to be there all the time. We have seen a pair of ravens there from time to time, and on one summer's evening we were treated to the extraordinary performance of the nightjar, whose song so closely resembles that of a two-stroke motor-cycle. We don't know what life the quarry pool contained, we couldn't get close enough to find out. But there must have been something of interest there. We once saw a heron standing motionless at the water's edge ... and herons don't waste time fishing barren waters.

And then came along the Official Tidiers Up, with Government money to spend.

We haven't been back to see what they have done. We daren't. We knew what their plans were. The quarry pool was declared 'dangerous'. It was to be pumped out, and the hole filled in by bulldozing the spoil heaps into it. The buildings were to be removed, the area 'landscaped', re-seeded and 'planted naturally' with (believe it or not) rowan, birch and ash. There would be plenty of space for parking cars, and the area was to become a 'picnic place'. I wonder what happened to the nightjar.

It is depressing to think that this is happening all over the British Isles in the name of 'conservation'.

But what has all this got to do with Hafod? Nothing. There aren't any 'conservationists' here.

The first animals we got to know were, of course, the mice. Very friendly creatures, the Hafod mice. They had gnawed their own little entrances at the corners of all the doors; holes in the plaster led through to their quarters, and they had emergency exits up all the chimneys. They seemed to want to be near us all the time, and when they weren't actually running around the floors or investigating the contents of boxes, they were rummaging noisily with the loose mortar in the walls, or playing football with bits of plaster across the ceiling. We cleared them out of the house by repairing the doors and blocking up their holes (after all, we try not to interfere with their nests in the garden, so why should they come and interfere with ours?) but we have failed to keep them out of the house structure. When a particularly heavy-footed creature bounded across the kitchen ceiling one evening, we thought we might be harbouring rats so Alan prised up a floorboard in the bedroom and put down a tin lid filled with poison. We soon regretted this. The creature who first ate of the poison took himself off and died in inaccessible obscurity somewhere under the bedroom floor. The stink filled the whole house, and we just had to live with it for three weeks. We only ever found one corpse. It was of a tiny pigmy shrew. We have never seen another one at Hafod. Did we kill the last one? No poison has ever been used at Hafod since then. (One curious thing about that lid of poison. When we finally removed it there was still about half the poison left, but it had been completely covered over with small stones and bits of plaster rubble—in a neat, carefully positioned pile.)

So we now put up with the things that rattle around in the walls and scurry up and down the rafters. It's only the gnawing of wood that worries us. To wake up in the night to sounds of strong teeth munching their way through the joists is not pleasant. But a good thump upon the floor usually sends them packing.

If we are somewhat unsociable towards the mice in the house, we at least try to make up for it by being nice to them in the garden. If they choose to nest in the compost heap (as they often do) we endeavour to leave them undisturbed until the family has scattered. And we don't get neurotic about a few nibbled root crops. Our mice and voles don't do a lot of damage. Only a few artichokes or potatoes at the edge of the plot get attacked, or a pea pod lying on the ground. As there is an abundance of their natural food around, why should they attack our crops? They have, admittedly, eaten nearly all of our yellow crocuses. So we grow white ones and purple ones instead. Apparently they don't taste so nice.

In return for our consideration, they amuse us with their antics. A daring bank vole who dashes out to join the birds feeding on the lawn causes comical confusion, and their twittering conversations and squeaking squabbles in the long grass are part of the sounds of summer.

The long-tailed field-mouse is a charming little chap, with huge eyes and large ears. He is a very pretty eater—picking up titbits with his front teeth and sitting back upon his haunches to eat in comfort. He also seems to be fairly tame. I don't know whether it is because they are trusting, short-sighted or just plain stupid, but it is possible to sit quite close to a field-mouse without disturbing it. I approached one once when he was feeding upon a small piece of cheese. He darted back into the wall as I squatted to watch him, but soon reappeared. I picked up the piece of cheese and held it between finger and thumb, with my hand resting upon the ground. Field-mouse approached cautiously and took the first nibble. Then, satisfied that all was in order, he sat back to enjoy his meal—resting his two front paws on my finger and thumb.

I think that we have more voles than mice. We have both bank voles and short-tailed ones, and these robust, trundling little rodents have not done much damage in the garden, although they have a bad reputation for attacking vegetables. They also, allegedly, eat the roots of young trees, and it is possible that we lost some of our young trees and hedging plants this way. But the only things we have actually seen them eating are blades of grass and young hawthorn leaves. Voles are not ones for eating out. Ever conscious of attack from above, they normally keep to their runs through the grass or along the hedge bottoms, occasionally nipping out in the open to grab a leaf or two to carry back home. Bank voles are nimble climbers and we have often seen them a foot or two off the ground running about inside a hawthorn hedge. With a hawthorn leaf in his mouth held aloft like a green umbrella, a bank vole running home through the hedge brings the world of Beatrice Potter into the garden.

But if Master Vole and Mistress Mouse are welcome characters in the tale of Hafod, Mister Mole certainly isn't. We wish he'd shuffle off into someone else's story. This energetic, thick-skinned underground tunnel borer has caused more havoc in our garden than any other creature, and all efforts to persuade him to go elsewhere have completely failed. He tunnels under the vegetable seed beds every year without fail, causing many seedlings to die, and he is continually undermining the bushes in the fruit garden. Young trees have been pushed out of the ground by a mole blundering past beneath them, and newly planted onions, shallots, peas and beans have suffered a similar fate. We have tried all the recommended deterrents, without resorting to gas or poison. There was the direct approach—like putting gorse and mole-traps in the runs (he just pushed these aside without noticing)—also the indirect approach—like planting empty bottles around the garden. The noise of the wind blowing across their tops was supposed to frighten him. Our mole didn't know this. He just carried on tunnelling, whilst the bottles filled up with water. Finally there was the mystical approach—like standing in the garden thinking kindly thoughts and asking the mole, very politely, if he would please go away. The failure of this method was probably my own fault. But then, *you* try thinking kindly thoughts when standing amidst the ruins of an undermined crop of young beetroot. I can remember asking the mole to go away ... but I don't think my language was very polite.

Then one day I caught him. I happened to be standing on the lawn, looking idly at a flower bed, when I noticed the ground moving. There was a rhythmical surging movement of the soil and I knew that a mole was working there, just below the surface. Without moving my feet I dropped to a crouch and squatted there with hands poised. When I judged that the mole was near enough to the surface for me to reach, I plunged my hands into the loose soil and heaved upwards. And there he was: struggling in confusion amidst the dirt. I seized him in both hands.

I was immediately impressed with his strength and agility. He was squirming and writhing with powerful body thrusts, and I had to hold him quite tightly and keep changing my grasp to maintain a grip on the smooth velvety fur. He was perfectly clean. Somehow I had expected a dirt groveller to be dirty, but his coat was short, dense, smoky black and without flaw, blemish or mud. He had a pointed snout and large feet with tiny needle-like claws. And these feet were on the go all the time—making strong plunging breast-stroke movements. What should I do with him? Why, kill him of course! How? I could smash in his head with a stone. Ugh, no. Too messy. Strangle him then. I wasn't sure. I wandered about the garden, undecided. He was getting extremely difficult to hold, so I bundled him up in my pinafore. In seconds his feet had torn through the cloth, so I hugged him to me and made for the field.

I couldn't do it. I knew perfectly well that I couldn't do it. I scrambled up the hill towards Charlie, then dropping to my knees again I tumbled the mole out of my pinny. His snout went into the grass and his feet moved forward. With two plunges of his front feet, he tore through the roots and into the soil. I sat back and watched him. The powerful muscles rippled in his velvety back as he lunged forward into the earth. Then slowly he disappeared. As his rounded backside vanished into the ground I gave a tweak to the ridiculous little tail. 'And don't come back!' I shouted. But he did. I'll bet he was back in the garden not long after me.

This episode seems to prove that I have not the courage of my convictions. I believe that no animal or plant should be killed needlessly, but that we are morally entitled to hunt and kill any animal that really threatens our food. But when it came to the crunch I couldn't do it. I don't think that Alan is any better. He delights in watching the chase-me-round-the-gorse-bushes games of the rabbits upon the hillside, but threatened death by any means to the persistent one who kept breaking into our garden and eating the nine-star broccoli. Muttering something about the tastiness of rabbit stew, he set a couple of snares in appropriate places, and we discussed the way that rabbit should be killed, skinned and prepared for the pot. Armed with a cudgel I would go out and inspect the snares at regular intervals—talking jocularly of seeing-what-we've-caught-for-dinner, but secretly hoping the snares would be empty. They always were. What's more, I began to suspect that Alan had set them in such a way that they could never even impede the progress of a passing rabbit, much less ensnare it. Anyway, the rabbit finally got bored with broccoli and took himself off. So we brought the snares back to the house, and pretended to be cross about not getting our rabbit stew.

Fortunately for us, the balance of nature is maintained at Hafod without our assistance. The stoat and weasel see to it for us.

I can't say that I'm very fond of the weasel. Long and thin, with a short tail, it looks like an oversized worm trotting about on four legs. Not an attractive creature. As its small size enables the weasel to pursue voles, mice and moles right to the end of their runs I must accept that weasel is doing us a good service in his dirty work underground. But I still don't like him. The stoat, on the other hand, is lovable. He moves gracefully—almost like a squirrel—stopping frequently to sit back, front paws held aloft whilst he quizzically sniffs the air. A stoat is full of curiosity. Once on a winter's day I stood motionless in the garden watching one; and he was watching me. Merging with the snowy scene in his coat of ermine, he came closer and closer, eyeing me with puzzled interest, and stopping to sniff the air every now and then. He came within two feet of me, then—deciding that I was of no further interest—turned aside and went on his way. I know that the stoat has habits as nasty as the weasel's, and will kill any creature who gets in his way just for the hell of it. He is a rogue, but a charming rogue. A stoat lived in the back-kitchen wall when we first moved into Hafod. I used to watch his comings and goings from the wash-up window. Unfortunately, the repair of the back-kitchen wall meant the stoat's eviction, but he has since taken up quarters in the bank alongside the front garden. His lair in the wall was quite a charnel house —including remains of birds, rabbits, and a skull and jaw-bone which we think was that of a rat.

The trouble with this policy of live-and-let-nature-do-the-killing is that although I'm prepared to turn a blind eye to the stoat's slaughter of the small mammals, I am liable to get upset when he turns his attention to the birds. During nesting season we go to extraordinary lengths to try and protect them. On the whole I think that the birds are more in danger from marauding farm cats than from stoats or weasels, but once, whilst in the middle of making bread, I had to rush out with dough-covered hands to chase a stoat away from the pied wagtail's nest.

Our most impressive carnivore didn't reveal himself until we had been at Hafod for a few years. One snowy winter's afternoon I was looking out of the kitchen window when I saw this huge cat-like creature. It appeared from the direction of the shippen, and it leapt upon the low wall surrounding the lawn, pausing at the top to look over its shoulder at me. Its colouring was rather like that of a tabby cat, but its back was very wide, and it had a thumping great bushy tail. There were distinctive markings upon its face, and a nasty anti-social look in its eyes. I hadn't the remotest idea what it was. When it moved off it went with the sinewy grace of a stoat. Our reference book on wild animals identified it for us. A polecat. And —according to the book—polecats are likely to take up residence during winter in deserted farm buildings. The shippen? We investigated. The back door of the shippen was broken at the bottom, so access for a polecat was quite possible. We cautiously went in, and there, in a dark corner behind some stacked timber we found a 'nest' of dried grass and bracken, surrounded with the debris of countless meals: bones of birds, and beasts, and a hedgehog skin. We withdrew hastily. The polecat might come back—and we didn't want to be caught prying. Several summers later we got around to repairing the shippen door—reasonably confident that the polecat could accommodate himself elsewhere. The ruined pigsty would be cosy enough, and there were several other corners around the place that could afford shelter. We haven't seen him lately, but he's still here somewhere. A few weeks ago a neighbour was passing the cottage late at night and was startled to see this large creature crossing his path. He said that it was the biggest polecat he had ever seen. We are not surprised; with comfortable quarters and an inexhaustible supply of hares, rabbits, rats, mice, voles and moles, it was probably also the healthiest and happiest one he had ever seen!

Wild cats are a problem. Not *real* wild cats, but farm cats that have taken to the hills. We have generally managed to keep them off the premises, but one year a female made a nest in the bracken on the hillside, and we didn't know anything about it until the day she marched proudly through the garden with her litter of three kittens. We shooed them away successfully, with the exception of one tiny all-black fury who decided that Hafod was to be his hunting ground. Whether we liked it or not, he was staying. He spent most of the time hunting in the long grass, and when we came across him he would just stand there—all of four inches off the ground— tiny paws spread wide, scruffy little back humped in fury, eyes a pair of hard blue beads of challenge, while he spat and hissed threats of savage aggression. Kitty was prepared to take on all comers. We were helpless. My instincts were to put out milk and food for him—try to tame him. But this would not be fair. We had tamed so many of the birds. In the end we decided to ignore him; treat him as another wild animal and leave him to his own devices. Kitty took up residence in a cardboard box underneath the caravan. We no longer tried to chase him away, but he eyed us warily from a distance. He was a very patient mouser. He would sit motionless upon a small stone wall, staring down at the ground, and he seemed to take no notice when birds came near. I began to hope that he might develop into an exclusively mouse-eating cat. But he didn't have a chance to develop into anything. One morning we found him lying beside his cardboard box. Spread-eagled upon the ground, with his little head at an awkward angle, Kitty was dead. His neck was bitten clean through. Polecat? Stoat, weasel or rat? Kitty hadn't stood a chance. But he'd had a go; it was obvious from the challenging position of those spread-eagled front paws that Kitty—weighing maybe six ounces—had gone down fighting.

Because we move through the garden carefully, and because we get so few visitors, the animals and birds of Hafod have become less wary. They are never in much of a hurry to get out of our way, and we are always prepared to drop what we are doing to sit and watch them. In this way we have got to know many of them personally, and we can sometimes tell what they are thinking and feeling. As well as the normally accepted emotional displays of sex attraction, anger, defence and greed, we have also witnessed embarrassment, worry, bad temper, compassion, humour, huffiness and grief. We believe that any human emotion can also be felt by an animal or bird. I don't know about insects and reptiles.

We are not naturalists. But the scientific approach is not the only one. We are, admittedly, anthropomorphists—and can justify our views.

I am interested to read a clinical description of the bank vole's size, shape and habits, but I can learn a lot more about it by sitting in the garden and watching. We once saw a bank vole trundling along the path in front of the house with her baby. Baby was skipping ahead, investigating here and there in the manner of all young things, when it suddenly came upon the ventilation grille we had fixed in the wall bottom for the underfloor draught to the parlour fire. This grille (it was an abandoned flat grate bottom) had bars that were spaced apart just wide enough for baby bank vole to squeeze through.

So he did. Mother bank vole scuttled up to the grille but was unable to get through the bars. Chittering with anger and frustration she poked her nose between the bars, ran back and forth in front of the grille, stretched up on her hind legs and pawed it—whilst baby, presumably, carried on exploring beneath the house. Mother's agitated cries eventually brought the baby squeezing back through the bars. As soon as he emerged, Mother gave him a swinging clout over the head with her front paw, then pushed him with her nose back on-to the path. Baby scuttled down the path with Mother close behind, pushing him with her nose and chittering angrily. I know just how she felt, and I've a good idea what she was saying.

Do hedgehogs maintain motherly instincts from one season to the next? I have never read that they do. But we once had one that seemed to. One winter we discovered a tiny hedgehog (obviously one of a late litter) who had chosen to hibernate in the tangle of suckers and dead leaves at the base of a lilac bush. When spring came we watched for baby to come out of hibernation—but he didn't stir. Apparently he hadn't sur-vived the winter. From traces on the lawn we knew that an adult hedgehog was out and about once more, so we put out a small aluminium-foil dish of bread and milk for it. (We had been in the habit of doing this the previous year, and were often rewarded with the sight of mother and young family feeding greedily and noisily upon their supper of bread and milk.) We waited the first evening, and saw a large hedgehog come to feed at the dish. But it didn't eat all the bread and milk, and turned aside to explore the garden. The next morn-ing we found the foil dish, with its contents spilled, tangled up in the suckers of the lilac where the dead baby hedgehog lay. We assumed that the wind had blown it there. The fol-lowing night we again put out the dish filled with bread and milk, but didn't stop to watch for the hedgehog. In the morn-ing the dish had gone from the lawn. Once again it was in the lilac bush ... only this time it had been dragged through all the suckers and dead leaves and had been deposited, upside down, on top of the little corpse.

We have never seen a badger at Hafod. In fact, the only

badgers I have ever seen have been dead ones—beside the road. My brother-in-law, who was a taxi driver, came across a pair of badgers in the middle of a deserted country road late one night. One badger was lying there, and the other refused to move away as he drove his taxi past. So he stopped a little way down the road and walked back to investigate. He could see that the badger lying in the road was dead. Its mate was running around the body poking, sniffing and crying aloud. Its cries varied from piteous whimpers to agonized squeals. My brother-in-law stood within a few feet of the badger, but he was ignored. He turned and went back to his taxi. There was nothing else he could do. No one who witnessed a scene like that could believe that animals are unable to feel grief.

We cannot claim to know any insect or reptile personally, but we have benign feelings towards all of them. Frogs, toads, lizards, ladybirds and other friends of the garden, are specially favoured, but I will even allow that slugs, leatherjackets and wire-worms have their rights. (After all, they were here first.) I can't bring myself to kill them, so they are chucked aside to carry on their affairs in the rough grass. (How one could cope with a philosophy like this in a suburban garden, where the only place to chuck them is in your neighbour's garden, I don't know.) I have not always had this reverence for life. Large moths and spiders that came into my childhood home were always slaughtered. Why? I never stopped to ask that question. Now I question everything. Moths and spiders are caught as gently as possible and put outside. Only house flies are killed. A tiny beetle that lands upon my forearm in the garden is something to be wondered at—not swiped at. I watch its progress along my skin, and find it incredible that such a tiny being can have a brain controlling functions of flying, crawling, breathing, eating, reproducing, fighting— and who knows what else! I waste time at the spring pool with blades of grass rescuing flies and bees from drowning, then I watch as they carefully and daintily unstick their sodden wings and wipe around their heads and faces with legs like threads of black cotton. A large fuzzy caterpillar galloping down the path will be removed to a safe feeding ground amongst the nettles. If he stays on the path, blackbird will catch him, and I want him to develop into a handsome garden tiger-moth, with crimson, cream and chocolate-brown wings. Have you ever heard a caterpillar chewing? If you get close enough, you can hear the steady munch, munch of its jaws.

The blackbird is a remorseless predator upon the lower orders in the garden. He fishes for tadpoles, will seize young frogs, and on one occasion I saw the female blackbird snatch a lizard from the rocks at the spring, only about sixteen inches away from me. The lizard's tail was snapped off in the fight, but the rest of him—still struggling—was carried off to be fed to a nest of young ones. I can't think how they managed it. (We suspect that our only newt met with a similar fate.)

Lizards have intelligent eyes. The eyes of mice, and some birds, are round black buttons—bright and expressionless, like a doll's eyes, but a lizard has thoughtful eyes. According to our reference books, lizards are uncaring for their offspring. When they are born the young are 'deposited anywhere', and the mother 'exhibits no interest or concern in her progeny'. But they seem to be gregarious creatures. We have seen parties of them together, young and old, basking in the sunshine; running over each other, lying touching each other. Perhaps there is a community concern for the young. I once rescued a lizard from the water bucket. I don't know how long he had been struggling there, but he was exhausted when I lifted him out, and he lay for some time on my hand gradually recovering. After a while he lifted his head and looked up at me, with a puzzled expression—as if he was wondering what on earth I was, and why I had rescued him. I nudged him with my thumb, and he scuttled away.

Dragonflies are fascinating creatures. Small ones, in bright jackets of red, green or blue, dart and hover near the flowers at the springhead. We also occasionally see large black and yellow striped ones. Our commonest butterfly is the orange-tip. We see them in parties around the garden, and they do not 'disappear' in the evening as the others seem to, but fall asleep just where they are, hanging on to a plantain, or daffodil, or somesuch. They seem to be able to withstand a night of high winds and rain, and one morning we came across a group of nine of them hanging from forget-me-nots, and covered in early morning dew.

I think that the most astonishing insect we have seen at Hafod is the humming-bird hawk-moth. One day I watched a pair of them hovering over the sage bushes. With wings just a blur of orange and brown, and with long tongues delicately probing each blossom, it was difficult to decide whether they were moths or sprites.

We try to identify all the moths and butterflies we see, but it is not always easy with the nondescript ones. We will, perhaps, find a likely illustration in the book, but may be put off by the text that assures us that either this particular insect has never been seen in Wales, or that it feeds on plants that we know do not grow around here. However, some moths and butterflies are so startling that it is not possible to make a mistake. Take the comma butterfly, for example. Two of these were feeding quietly upon our blackberry bushes one day last September. With their scalloped and raggedly notched wings bearing the silver 'comma' on their undersides, they were unmistakable. But, according to our book, the comma butterfly has not been seen further west than Worcestershire, and they are not supposed to like blackberries. Delighted at being able to add an original comment to the known facts of the comma butterfly, we made an appropriate addendum to the book.

A long summer's day, that ends with the arrival of the dusk moths and the pipistrelle bats, sometimes finds me scurrying around to sweep the kitchen, fetch the water and prepare a meal. 'But what on earth have you been *doing* all day?' Alan will ask.

10. BIRDS

My mother taught me about birds. I have known her turn off
the radio because it was interfering with her enjoyment of the
blackbird's song; an appreciation of avian music not readily
shared by a juvenile who wanted to hear *Dick BARton—
Special AGent*—but at least it meant that the blackbird's
song, once heard, was not likely to be forgotten. At my
mother's knee I also learned to identify song thrushes, sparrows, starlings, robins, chaffinches, blue tits and (surprisingly)
dunnocks. But an enthusiastic and enquiring interest was not
aroused until the day on Mendip when I was convinced that
I had seen an eagle. With the aid of a book from the library
I was able to identify it as my first buzzard.

Since living at Hafod I have learned to identify many more
species (see Appendix A) and the birds that come to live in
the garden get special consideration. To a large extent this
means simply leaving them alone. During the nesting season
we keep strictly to the paths and don't go prying around in
long grass or bushes. Where they choose to nest is their business. We have provided nesting-boxes for the starlings, blue
and great tits and robins, preserved holes in walls for the
wagtails, wheatears and redstarts—and will go to the rescue
of any bird that seems to need it—but we keep out of their
way as much as possible. Some of them, however, do not seem
particularly anxious to keep out of *our* way. Dunnocks, mistle-
thrushes, redpolls, blackbirds and meadow pipits have nested
low down in the Sitka spruces alongside the spring path, so
that we could not fail to see what was going on each time we
passed with buckets. And a wren once insisted on building a
nest upon a beam in the outhouse just a couple of feet above

our bicycles—which were used many times each week. The nestlings' first flight took them down onto the brake cables; very handy perching places for tiny feet.

Wrens are here all the year round. We seem to have two pairs normally nesting with us—one couple in a hedge in the front garden and the other using an outbuilding. Wrens seem to be singing all the time, and there is surely no more passionate singer than a ferocious little wren declaring his territorial rights. With uplifted beak, erect tail and a body quivering with the urgency of it all, he pirouettes like a clockwork toy. When the young ones make their first exploratory flights into the garden they tend to keep together. And what a fussy, ticking, squeaking bunch they are too. If you pass by the bush where they are sitting, there will be an explosion of tiny wrens, hurtling away noisily in all directions. We do not know our wrens individually, so they carry on their affairs of fighting, courtship and the rearing of young without us being aware of their dramas and tragedies.

It has never been our intention to strike up an acquaintance with any particular bird. It is much more comfortable to have a vague affection for a garden full of assorted species. With the love of an individual bird comes a feeling of responsibility for its welfare; concern for its comfort; a gnawing worry if it is missing for a few days and grief when it dies. We shy away from such emotional entanglements ... we do not wish to get involved. But every year our good intentions founder. For birds are like people. With some of them you can have an easy-going here-today-gone-tomorrow relationship, but others become part of your life for a while, and you never forget them.

Pinny was the first. She was a great tit who came to us during our first winter at Hafod. Every morning I used to sprinkle oatmeal along the top of a low wall near the kitchen window, and I noticed that the first birds to arrive were always a pair of great tits. I took no particular notice of these birds, and I didn't hang about over the job of food distribution. It was thrown down hurriedly and I retreated to the warmth of the kitchen to watch. Then one morning the pair of great tits flew down to the wall before I had actually scattered the oatmeal. So, just for fun, I didn't scatter it. I pulled out a handful from the bag, then placed my hand flat upon the wall. To my utter astonishment one great tit hopped straight along the wall and onto my hand and began to feed with an unhurried nonchalance that took my breath away. I stood there, motionless and slowly freezing, whilst this delightful bird, with gentle feet, deliberately ate all the oatmeal upon my hand. The other great tit was hopping around about six inches away, churring crossly, and dashing in closer every now and then to pick up a crumb that fell from my hand to the wall.

This was the start of an emotional entanglement that was to last for six years.

We fed them on fat and peanuts as well as oatmeal and it soon became obvious which was the male and which was the female—from their behaviour as well as the slightly larger size and broad belly stripe of the male. Pinny was always completely trusting, and quite at ease when feeding from our hands. She flew to them without hesitation, ate daintily, and landed and took off with very gentle feet. Podger, her mate, had an entirely different personality. He only plucked up courage to come to our hands because he had seen Pinny do so. But he made a great fuss about it. Dashing in with great bluster, he would land with a clunk of clawed feet, grabbing what he could and making off with it straight away. We went to the door with peanuts as soon as we saw the birds at our window in the morning. If Podger arrived first he would sit on a nearby bush churring and chinking fussily until Pinny arrived to feed. He was probably kidding her that he was being a gentleman, but we know that he needed the reassurance of seeing her feed first.

The tits (both blue and great) do not normally nest at Hafod, and the nesting-boxes we put up are used by them only as roosting places during the winter and autumn. (Sparrows occasionally take them over during the nesting season.) The tits usually leave us around May and move downhill to the woodlands to nest, returning to us with their young in August. For two seasons a pair of blue tits nested in a hole in the rowan, and one year Pinny and Podger used a cavity in the outhouse, but we got the impression that they were doing so against their better judgement and that there was some deeply rooted urge to move off downhill that they should have been obeying. Unfortunately the very year that Pinny and Podger nested at Hafod, we were obliged to leave the cottage for much of the summer, so we weren't there to see what happened. When we returned in September there were no young great tits to be seen, and no Podger. Only Pinny was waiting for us—quiet, sad-eyed, and trusting as ever.

The following season another male great tit put in an appearance, but he was a timid shilly-shallying sort of fellow, and Pinny showed no interest in him. He followed her around for a while, and we referred to him as 'boy-friend', but we didn't think he was good enough for Pinny. And then Joe bounced in. Joe was the smartest, biggest, bravest great tit we had seen ... and he knew it. Strutting around, churring and piping loudly, he soon sent 'boy-friend' packing, and swept Pinny off her feet. There was no nonsense with Joe about feeding from the hand. He would have none of it. He sat and watched Pinny come for peanuts with an impassive go-ahead-if-you're-such-a-damn-fool attitude, and then waited for us to throw him one. Which we always did. What's more, he didn't wait patiently for us to come out in the morning. He came and hammered on the window for his peanut. If we were late getting up he would come and hammer at the bedroom window. If he couldn't see us in the kitchen or the bedroom he would go and peer in the parlour window. His first taps would be crisp and light. Then they would get harder and more impatient. If we didn't attend to him then, he would hammer in a fury that threatened to break the glass. We have shouted at him, cursed him, and chucked pot-holders and tea towels at the window in desperation. But nothing would stop Joe hammering on the window, except a peanut thrown out to him. And then he would snatch it up, glare at us, and go away churring something that sounded like 'And about time too!'

Pinny had no worries about bringing her young ones to us, and on one occasion she allowed her two offspring (Jenny and Bella) to stay and feed at Hafod all the winter. When Jenny and Bella came to Hafod they copied their mother in feeding from our hands without hesitation. They went to Alan first of all. Pinny flew to him to eat oatmeal, and her two squeaking, feather-fluttering youngsters joined her on his hand. He stood there grinning like an idiot whilst Pinny fed placidly, pretending to ignore her demanding offspring. She looked up at him once with an expression that he swears was meant to convey the fact that she knew what she was doing—and she went on ignoring the young ones. Eventually they got the idea, and they too began pecking oatmeal from his hand. After that they mobbed us whenever we set foot outside the door. They assumed that hands always contained something to eat, and any hand in the garden—be it lighting a pipe, handling secateurs, doing up a button, or scratching a head—was liable to have a pair of tiny feet come scrabbling over it searching for food.

Pinny had an unfailing memory. On one occasion we had to leave the cottage for five months and as soon as we returned we looked out for her. She came straight to us for a peanut, silently, and gently, with just a hint of reproach in her eyes. We only once saw her in a temper. It was at dusk on one winter's afternoon and she and Joe were having a row about something. She was hopping along the front hedge in the direction of her roost (a robin's nesting-box) with Joe following her, and they were quarrelling loudly. Pinny hesitated in the rowan just below her roost, turned around and gave Joe a final scold, then flew into the box. But Joe hadn't finished. He carried on hopping around in the hawthorn hedge, chinking loudly and kicking up a fuss. Then suddenly Pinny reappeared. She shot out of her box, a whirlwind of furious feathers. She flew at Joe chinking and piping shrilly. She pushed him out of the bush and chivvied him back along the hedge and then, with a final angry cascade of vituperation she flew like an arrow back to her box. We almost heard her slam the door. Joe, muttering sullenly to himself, took himself off down the hedge.

Pinny and Joe were inseparable companions for four years. When they sat together in a hedge they looked like matching pepper and salt pots. At all seasons of the year, if you saw the one, the other wouldn't be more than a few feet away. They were separated, eventually, by death.

In the late summer a couple of years ago we waited eagerly for Joe and Pinny to return with their brood. August came and went and then September. I refused to accept that they were not coming back. They were simply a bit late, I decided. Then one day in early October Joe returned. At first we didn't recognize him—he was in such a state. In an advanced stage of moult, he was practically bald, and the feathers upon his body were dull, loose and tatty. He didn't want to be seen, and spent most of the time silently skulking in the hedge. He came to the window and peered in occasionally, but when a peanut was thrown he picked it up quickly and disappeared without saying anything. He seemed defeated, dejected, spiritless and miserable. Joe's grief finally convinced me that the unthinkable had happened. Pinny was dead. It was many months before we could bear to mention her name.

During the winter Joe began to recover—even to the extent of tapping the window for his nuts again. But he didn't have the same fire and energy. In the following spring he called eagerly for a mate, but none came. So he flew away. And since then there have been no great tits at Hafod.

We have never really kept track of the Hafod blue tits. At the end of the summer there seem to be dozens of them around the place—flitting about the trees, hanging upside down on the kale leaves, fighting each other like schoolboys, pecking putty from the windows, and begging for peanuts. The only one we really got to know was called Booboo—and we were not even sure of Booboo's sex. We thought she was female because she had gentle manners like Pinny; but we couldn't be sure. Booboo roosted in a coconut shell we had fixed near the parlour window, almost touching the glass. She didn't mind the light from the window, nor the noise of the radio, but we had to be very careful when pulling the curtains. She curled up right at the far end of the shell, and all we could see was a little ball of fluff. Booboo came to our hands for peanuts with a gentle, unhurried confidence. Other blue tits followed her example, and three scruffy little urchins called Pip, Squeak and Wilfred, used to fight each other to get in first. (Pip was Booboo's mate.) Then more of the tits came to us for peanuts, and then we couldn't tell one from another. During that summer we had six or seven blue tits feeding from our hands, but the only ones we really knew by sight were Booboo and Pip.

Booboo was with us for four years. She died in a manner that is common enough to birds elsewhere, but a rarity at Hafod. She was struck by a passing vehicle. When Alan found the little corpse in the track outside the cottage we felt, with a sort of dreadful certainty, that it was Booboo. Neither of us had seen her since lunch that day. I found myself hoping that it was one of the others (we had sixteen blue tits with us at the time), but that evening at dusk our fears were confirmed. There was no little ball of fluff in the coconut shell.

A curious thing happened on the day of Booboo's death. During that particular summer Booboo and Pip had been the only blue tits who were feeding from our hands; the others would only take peanuts that were tossed to them. But on the evening of the day that Booboo died Alan found himself besieged by a crowd of them, each one coming to his hand to take a peanut, and, thereafter, we carried on hand-feeding them for the rest of the year.

The relationship that develops between us and the birds we hand feed is rather like that between the householder and the carol singer. We give, in the first place, because it delights us to—and they are suitably grateful. But then they become more demanding, and we find them a nuisance. We give in order to get rid of them; we even try to avoid them. The birds will expect to be fed anywhere at any time. Whether we are digging vegetables, mixing cement, carrying water, or sitting in the privy—they will come and churr at us impatiently and expect the peanut to be produced. We feel we dare not venture outside without a quantity of peanut 'ammunition' in our pockets. If we are caught without any we feel morally obliged to leave what we are doing to return to the house and fetch some. Sometimes we play tricks on them. Alan once offered Pinny a handful of crumbled-up biscuit. She sorted through this for a second, looked up at him quizzically, then gave him a sudden sharp peck on the hand, and flew off to a nearby bush where she sat and scolded him. He apologized, produced a peanut, which she came and took, without saying anything further.

If we offer a handful of nuts to a bird, it will always sort them through in order to find the biggest—sometimes tossing small pieces over the side. If the nuts on the hand are of more or less equal size, the bird is in a dilemma. It will pick up first one, then another, trying hard to make a decision. If the nuts are broken into small bits, it will stand there and eat until it has polished off the lot. (In this manner we have managed to photograph a few of them.) Some birds would like to take peanuts from our hands, but are too nervous. They are torn between greed and fear, and their perplexity is amusing to watch. A peanut held on a hand within a few inches of a nervous bird will be regarded by a covetous eye, whilst the feathers on the bird's head will visibly rise in fear. Sometimes they will react to a proffered hand by looking away in embarrassment. As I approach with outstretched hand, an embarrassed bird will peck the twig on which he is sitting, give himself a quick preen, or simply gaze up into the air offhandedly. These taunts and lures of ours never work. If a bird wishes to come to the hand he will come without cajoling. If he doesn't then he will *never* come.

Chaffinches refuse to feed from our hands, yet they will feed within inches of our feet. We usually have two pairs nesting with us and, once again, the house seems to be the territorial boundary between the couple in the front garden and the pair that take over the back garden and field. The nest of a chaffinch is surely one of the neatest and prettiest nests made. It is also a sound bit of engineering. A chaffinch once built her nest in a rather exposed and somewhat threadbare elder tree just outside our bedroom window. It was secured between six slender twigs, and when a gale blew up one night we feared for her safety. Next morning, with the wind gusting occasionally to storm force, Mrs. Chaffinch was still there, upon her violently rocking nest. With only her head and tail visible the little bird was facing into the wind and riding out the storm. This weather lasted non-stop for three days and nights, during which time a mistle-thrush's nest came to grief, and the redpoll's nest was blown clean out of a Sitka spruce tree. But at the end of it all, the nest of the chaffinch was still there; a little tattered, but intact. What's more it didn't finally disintegrate until two winters later.

All young birds are charming, but baby chaffinches are the funniest. Whilst waiting for their parents to feed them they adopt a curious sideways bobbing motion, which speeds up in tempo as a beak full of food looms near. The parent chaffinch sometimes appears to have difficulty in getting food down the throat of her agitated offspring whose head is jerking from side to side with the speed of a fully wound clockwork toy. As soon as the young ones leave the nest they are brought to the back door, or the kitchen window to be introduced to oatmeal, cheese and peanuts.

A couple of years ago our population of chaffinches was depleted by some mysterious cause that we have never fathomed. We knew that something was wrong when the two males (Sergeant and Billy) both came in the front door and sat around dozing upon the mat. This was in August, and both had young families to feed and territory to guard. (They had been fighting and swearing at each other the previous day.) During fine summer weather we normally have the kitchen door open all day, and it is quite common for birds to trot in to seek us out, but we had never seen them sitting around moping like this. Peanuts we tossed to them were looked at blearily for a minute, then eyes would close again. They were obviously feeling very ill. Occasionally Billy would hop further into the kitchen, and once he approached Alan who was sitting in the stairs. He hopped slowly across until he was standing between Alan's feet, then he looked up at him with appealing, miserable eyes. 'Do something, can't you!' he seemed to be saying. We felt helpless and useless. When dusk fell we decided that we had better put them in an outhouse. We didn't feel that we could leave them shut in the kitchen in case they recovered when we weren't there, panicked, and possibly injured themselves on the hot stove. We picked them both up easily enough, but when we put them down upon an old coat in the outhouse they suddenly seemed to get strength from somewhere and they both flew straight out of the door. Billy returned instantly to the kitchen, whilst Sergeant sat on the window-sill and looked miserably in through the glass. We decided that we had better make arrangements to accommodate them inside. We rescued Sergeant from the window ledge, placed him on folded-up newspaper on the kitchen floor and placed a large oval wire-mesh meat cover over him. We made a similar arrangement for Billy, but used a wire-mesh fire guard placed face down and butted up against a wall. Both put their heads beneath their wings and settled down for the night. We hoped that in the peace and warmth of the kitchen they would perhaps recover. But the next morning both were dead. Could they have been poisoned? This seemed to be the most likely answer, but the nearest possible source of 'dressed' seed was a recently ploughed and re-sown field a quarter of a mile away. Or was it something we had been feeding them? We bought the oatmeal at a shop where rat poison was often left lying around. Could the oatmeal have become contaminated? Or were they suffering from some natural disease? We decided that we should try and find out. We carefully packed up the two corpses, together with a sample of the oatmeal, and also a portion of the newspaper upon which each bird had died. (The paper had become soiled with a greenish fluid.) We wrote a letter of explanation, and addressed the package to the Royal Society for the Protection of Birds at Bedfordshire. We marked the package 'Urgent Specimens for Analysis ... First Class Post'. I was down at the local post office by 9.15 a.m. and, having explained the position to the postmistress, she promised to pass on a message to the collecting postman who was due in fifteen minutes' time. I was later assured that the message of urgency had been passed down the line, and that the package was on the London train that morning. It must have arrived at the Society's office the next day. And there, apparently, it stayed—for the next three days before it was sent off to the Ministry of Agriculture Veterinary Laboratories for examination. When the Ministry report came through to us it was revealed that the corpses were a week old before the Ministry had a chance to examine them. Not surprisingly they stated that decomposition was too far advanced for any conclusion to be reached. They also stated that the sample of oatmeal and the piece of newspaper that had been referred to in our letter never reached them.

Meanwhile chaffinches were continuing to die at Hafod. A couple of starlings and dunnocks also perished and, finally, our male blackbird. So we just buried them all.

Nigger, the blackbird, took longer to die than the chaffinches. He was moping for a fortnight, and we watched him getting weaker and weaker. He was feeding his third brood of the season at the time, but on the last few days of his illness he was obviously finding their demands too much for him. He spent much of his time trying to avoid them—finding a ledge or a bush out of their way where he could sit and doze. The day came when Nigger spent many hours just sitting on the lawn sheltering from the wind behind the low stone wall. I saw him eyeing the pan of water on top of the wall. It was obvious that he wanted a drink, but couldn't raise the strength to fly up to it. I carried out a saucer of water and he took a long drink. He refused all food. When dusk fell we knew that we should have to help him. If he stayed on the ground all night he would fall a victim to stoat or weasel. We put a small wooden box on its side on the lawn near the wall, weighted it down with a stone, and lined it with a bit of cloth. Then we came back to the kitchen, and watched from the window. Just before nightfall Nigger went into the box. Alan slipped out and placed a piece of wire-mesh in front of the open side, and held it in place with a stone. We knew that Nigger was going to die that night but at least he would die in peace.

11. MORE BIRDS

With the death of Nigger, his son Scrit came back to take over the territory. Scrit had been born the previous year. He was an unusually saucy and charming juvenile and had shown no fear of us whatsoever. He would come begging for food at the wash-up window. We tried hard to refuse him because we knew that Nigger would not allow him to remain in the garden and we didn't want him to get the idea that life was easy. But Scrit had winning ways. He would lightly tap the window, and if we shouted 'No!' he would look very sad and open his mouth wide. If this had no effect he would look even sadder and stand on one leg. This gambit usually brought us to the back door with currants. If these tricks failed Scrit would squat down on the window sill and sing us a sad little song, very quietly. Scrit didn't always come to us to beg for food, sometimes he just seemed to want company. He would often come and sit on the mat just inside the front door, and sing this quiet little warbling sub-song. If we offered him currants when he didn't particularly want them he would perhaps eat just one, to please us but leave the rest on the mat.

Scrit is now the Hafod blackbird, and his practice warbles on our mat have developed into a full varied tuneful song. But this year his territory is being threatened by another blackbird and Scrit, we fear, is no fighter. He made some half-hearted runs at this invader when he first appeared but only now, when Scrit is feeding his second brood, is he actually fighting the stranger. But it's too late. The stranger has already got a wife ensconced in our front hedge and he is obviously going to defend her position down to the last claw and beak. We are now constantly running out into the garden to separate them, which pleases Scrit—who just stands to one side—but baffles the stranger who is obliged to fly off screaming abuse. Having cottoned on to the idea that we are prepared to fight his battles for him, Scrit is now avoiding actual contact with the stranger and instead comes to the kitchen window and lets out a high-pitched scream when our presence is required in his defence. We are hoping that eventually they will agree to share the territory.

As well as fending off this stranger, Scrit is also trying to drive away his first brood. But he's having trouble with one of them. This youngster has taken to hanging about the wash-up window, opening his beak in a request for food, standing on one leg and singing a little song. With a feeling of this-is-where-we-came-in, we try to explain to him that life is hard and that he must go away and dig worms. When we do slip him a currant or bit of cheese it is with an exhortation not to tell his Dad. We call him The Scritling.

We talk to our birds like other people talk to their dogs. This is quite a harmless exercise in one's own garden, but liable to cause misunderstanding elsewhere. I once stopped at the cross roads beyond the village to have a conversation with a pair of crows. As I pedalled off I caught sight of a farmer sitting on his stationary tractor and peering at me over the top of a hedge. He was wearing an expression of absolute horror—and obviously thought that I should be riding a broomstick, not a bicycle.

Does a bird's song reflect the quality of its habitat? When we first came to Hafod there was very little cover for the birds and the song of the currently resident blackbird was a very feeble effort, consisting of three notes and a strangulated squawk. The quality of the singing has been getting progressively better, and Scrit has a wide range of melodious phrases that he repeats, then varies with tuneful originality.

And whilst raising questions about bird songs—whatever happens to the cuckoo's in June? He seems to wear it out with over-use in April and May, so that when June comes all he can manage is the 'cuck' part followed by a wheezy squeak.

We have no set method of naming our birds. Their names are suggested to us in a variety of ways. Nigger was so called because he sang from the top of a woodpile, and Joe was Joe because, well, he was so *obviously* a Joe. All male sparrows are known to us as Reynolds, after a rotund clownish acquaintance of ours, and anyone who has watched a pied wagtail high-stepping it around the water's edge will understand why we call our female Mrs. Kinky Boots. Lumpus was a mistle-thrush who was afraid to leave the nest. Day after day he would sit there, a little lump in the nest, high in the fork of the ash tree, totally ignoring all the pleas and scolds of his parents. One day he ventured up along the bough a couple of feet and we thought that at last he was going to take off. Both parents arrived. They chattered at him, flew around him, then sat on either side and scolded him noisily. We could see Lumpus shrinking under the parental blast—but he stayed there, a hunched up little lump of misery. His parents flew off, and Lumpus began to look longingly back at the safety of the nest below him. After a while he started shuffling sideways back to it, one foot at a time. The last few inches were done in a rush and Lumpus plopped back into the nest with relief. The parents continued to come to the nest and feed him. Then one day we noticed that the nest was empty. Lumpus, it seemed, had finally made it. The following year a mistle-thrush nested only 3 feet off the ground in one of our Sitka spruce trees. Was this the nest of Lumpus, the bird who was afraid of heights?

Sometimes a bird will choose a most unsuitable site for a nest. The pied wagtails were particularly stupid one year. We have provided them with two nesting-holes—one in the gable end of the shippen, and one in the wall of the outhouse. They normally use first the one and then the other during the nesting season. But one year Mrs. Kinky Boots chose to ignore these cavities and set up home in a pile of timber only about 2 feet 6 inches off the ground. One day I heard cries of distress and agitation coming from the vicinity of the timber pile and I saw both parent wagtails hovering over the rough ground near the nest. I dashed across and obviously arrived just in time. A farm cat, crouching low in the grass, gave me a malevolent yellow-eyed glare before turning and streaking off. It had been about 18 inches from the crevice in the timber where five anxious little faces peered out. But the cat would obviously come back. What could we do to protect the wagtails? Alan made a bulging shield of 2-inch mesh wire-netting, which we hoped was big enough for the birds to get through, yet strong enough to withstand cat's paws. He stapled this shield over the crevice in the timber, hoping that the whole lot wouldn't come toppling down as he cautiously wielded the hammer. The little ones just stared at him with unblinking eyes, whilst the two parents watched, silently, from the wall a few feet away. We retreated to the kitchen, and looked out of the window. We knew that with this amount of interference, the birds might desert their young in the nest. But if we had done nothing, then they would have perished at the paws of cat anyway, so we decided the chance had to be taken. After a short while, Mrs. Kinky Boots flew towards the nest with some food in her mouth. She hovered uncertainly in front of the wire-netting screen, then retreated to the wall, baffled. Then she came again. This time, after a moment's hovering she went through the wire-netting. We breathed sighs of relief ... and got on with whatever it was that we were doing before the flap had started.

Eventually, all the young wagtails flew successfully from the nest, and we hoped that Mrs. Kinky Boots had learned her lesson and that she would return to the official wagtail quarters for her second brood. But did she? The silly creature chose the window-ledge in the long wall of the shippen—again only about two feet off the ground. But at least it was closer to the house this time—in full view of the kitchen window in fact. She made her nest, laid her eggs and hatched them without incident. Then one day we heard the hullabaloo again. This time a stoat was the marauder. Standing up on his hind legs, his front paws upon the window-ledge, he was peering into the nest with great interest. I dashed out to drive him off, and he bounded for cover into the low stone wall beside the lawn. I leaped onto the wall and started clumping up and down. The stoat shot out from the other side of it and raced away to the field. He must have had quite a shock, because he didn't come back. Which is just as well. We could have devised no wire-netting screen that would have allowed access to the wagtails, yet kept out a stoat. However, we decided that the nest ought to have some form of protection, and Alan fixed some 2-inch mesh wire-netting to a wooden frame which completely covered the window aperture. The frame was held in position by some heavy pieces of timber and a crow-bar wedged into the ground. This would keep out cats, if nothing else. Once again the parents soon mastered the knack of passing through the wire-netting, and when the time came for the young ones to fly they emerged without mishap —although we did have an anxious moment when one of the young ones got his long legs tangled up momentarily in the wire-netting.

After the nesting season the wagtails move off. They are never with us during the winter. House sparrows and starlings also stay here only during nesting time. As soon as the year starts closing in they move off to more civilized parts.

Starlings are the most entertaining of clowns. Their nesting-box is in the ash tree facing the kitchen window and we are able to watch their domestic goings-on from start to finish. We get the impression that Mrs. Starling (Girlie) is very houseproud, and most particular about her furnishings. Her husband (Boyoh) is an amiable chap and always prepared to lend a hand, but doesn't seem to get the hang of doing things the way she wants them. Nesting materials are gathered mainly by Girlie, and she spends a lot of time in the box arranging them. Occasionally, when she is out of the way, Boyoh will do his bit and bring in a length of straw or bundle of grasses, but when she comes back there's hell to pay. Squawking at him in fish-wife language, she pulls out all the things he has brought and chucks them out of the box. He shrugs his shoulders and takes himself off to a nearby twig where he will chortle, whistle, pop and gurgle at the sunshine, whilst flapping his wings in accompaniment.

House sparrows occasionally nest in a box we put up for blue tits. As the tits have never used it for nesting we enlarged the hole a little so that the male sparrow (Reynolds) could get his corpulent shape in and out easier. Sparrows are the most unselfconscious lovemakers. The nesting box was provided with a perch where the two birds often sat side by side, and Reynolds the lecher spent most of the time leaping on and off his wife's back. She always looked bored with the whole performance. Occasionally she side-stepped and Reynolds, puffed up with passion, would land in a dishevelled heap beside her.

We have never been able to establish any sort of *rapport* with the sparrows or starlings. They use our facilities and will eat our food, but they don't want to know us. The starlings swear at me if I mow the lawn beneath their box, but generally speaking they ignore us. If we approach them they immediately fly away. We find this rather strange as the other Hafod birds are not scared of us. When we open the back door in the morning, a group of birds will come flying towards us to scrounge titbits. But the starlings and sparrows remain coldly aloof. They don't trust us. And I can't make up my mind whether this means that they are stupid or more intelligent than the others.

The sexiest female bird is undoubtedly the chaffinch. She will happily lift her skirts to all comers—not caring whether it is her husband or the other chap. When the birds come for peanuts, the female chaffinch is torn between greed and lust. She will make sure that she is at the head of the peanut queue, but at the first sign of a male chaffinch she will arch her back, lift her tail feathers and display an inviting backside. The male chaffinches, on the other hand, seem to be able to take it or leave it. When one does oblige her, he will approach with a curious sideways movement, and finally leap aboard with a rattling trill. But if there are peanuts around they are not interested in sex. I have seen a male chaffinch walk straight past the quivering rump of his girl friend, in order to steal her nut.

The dunnocks, normally quiet secretive little birds, also make love in public—on the lawn, or in the middle of the path—wherever he happens to catch up with her. Their sex chase is a non-stop game throughout the spring and summer; she coyly hopping away and he following up with a little flick of one wing at each step. The only other birds we have seen mating here are the swallows; and they prefer a barbed-wire fence for the job. Robins like privacy for the act of love, but he's a great exhibitionist over the courtship rituals—making a great show when bringing her titbits of flies and grubs. But once the nesting season is over he's a brute to her, and will never let her come near the tray of food in winter. Robin is the cad with a bunch of roses, only after One Thing.

We notice that our birds' 'table manners' vary tremendously. Blackbirds are the messiest eaters. Scrit chucks mud and leaves all over the place in his search for grubs, and then comes begging at the wash-up window with a face plastered in dirt, grass hanging from his beak and leaves stuck on his head. Dunnocks, on the other hand, feed with a neat precision, pecking away daintily at infinitesimal crumbs. Redpolls are charming to watch as they sit upon the path feeding prettily from the daisy plants. The seed-eating birds amaze us. It is incredible that a comparatively bulky bird—like a sparrow or linnet—can sit upon a stalk of grass and eat the seeds. The goldfinches have a particularly clever way of managing this feat. I once watched one sitting upon a stem of groundsel. He pulled another head of the plant towards himself, then trapped it under his foot and ate the seeds. Still standing on this, he pulled another stem towards himself and stood on it, and then another, until he was standing securely upon a strong platform of seeding groundsel heads. With fluffy seeds spewing out all around his beak, he munched away looking a picture of contentment.

The first of the summer visitors to arrive is the wheatear. When we see his white rump flashing up the hillside we know that the season has begun. They rarely come near the house, and they nest in the wall by the stable. Now, each day, we will be watching out for the others. Any day soon we will hear the song of the willow-warbler—a gentle, wistful cadence that startles us with delight when we first hear it each year, but that soon becomes just one of the happy threads of sound in the summer tapestry of song at Hafod. The willow-warblers build their nest near the house in the long grass of the wych-elm plot. They flit around the garden quite openly and do not seem to mind us being near them. Whinchats come to nest each year in a little patch of rough grass and young trees that we call 'whinchat patch'. They are wary little birds. He sits on guard upon the barbed-wire fence near the nest, and will tick nervously if we go too near. Goldcrests pass through Hafod at this time of the year. They have never nested with us, but pay our conifers an annual visit. Feeding busily amongst the branches, they do not mind how close we stand to watch them.

The swallows are boisterous, exuberant and don't give a damn. Alan has had his hair parted by them swooping across him in the garden—for no other reason than devilment. They set up home in the stable each year, usually after a minor fracas with the wren, who, given half a chance, will take over the swallows' nest if they are a bit late in arriving. Although the stable is theirs by ancient rights, this doesn't stop the swallows from exploring the rest of the buildings for a new site. We have even found them investigating inside the kitchen.

As the days grow warmer and lengthen, we lose track of the arrivals. Redpolls, pipits and whitethroats will be carrying food to their young in the nest before we realize that they have established themselves, and soaring ecstatic larks will be declaring part of the field out of bounds. A pair of partridge nest with us each year in the long grass and once (and once only) we accommodated corncrakes. Their strange rasping croak was part of the Hafod evensong for one season, but we never saw them, and they have never come again.

The songs of a summer's evening have a strange enchantment about them, very different from the fresh enthusiasm of the dawn chorus. In the garden the voices of chaffinch, robin, willow-warbler and blackbird predominate. But come up the hillside to the top of the field and the cries of the wilderness take over. To the north and east horizons the moorland stretches—a turbulent rolling sea of bell heather, ling and bog cotton, where the grouse stalk warily and a drumming snipe falls out of the sky in crazy loops. Here is the sad piping call of the golden plover and the mournful trill of the whimbrel. A high-flying pair of ravens *kronk* thoughtfully homewards.

From up here the cottage squats beneath you, in a cosy huddle of trees and garden. In front of the cottage the moorland slopes downwards, broken here and there with rocky outcrops, stretches of marshland and scrubby hawthorn and blackthorn trees. This is the haunt of the grasshopper warbler who trills without pause throughout a summer's evening, and the aerobatic lapwing who squeals plaintively as he carves up the sky. But principally, this is the country of the curlew.

What is there in the song of a curlew? All the sadness of a thousand tales with unhappy endings, all the yearnings of parted loved ones, the griefs of bereaved ones, the sighs for what might have been, and the longings for what cannot be. The song rises in a curve of liquid bubbling notes full of forlorn hope, then falls away in a dying cadence of sadness. The song of the curlew brings an ache to the heart, a lump to the throat and tears to the eyes.

The name of this land is Hiraethog. *Hiraeth* is that almost untranslatable Welsh word whose nearest English equivalent is longing or yearning.

The curlew is the bird of Hiraethog.

12. EARNING MONEY

Viewed from the the security of my office desk (complete with
its 9.0 a.m. to 5.0 p.m. chains and weekly pay-packet) the
world of the casual work-today, loaf-tomorrow idler seemed
unquestionably attractive. It was wrapped up with a sort of
gypsy-cum-vagabond give-to-me-the-life-I-love romantic haze
that started to evaporate slightly when I was handed my cards,
and fizzled out completely into a blue funk after a fortnight's
unemployment. Having been brought up to accept that regular employment was the natural order of things, I had previously never allowed the door of one job to close behind me,
without there being another doorway ready to step through
in front of me. As soon as the chains were thrown off, I
wanted them back again. Freedom frightened me. I was
ready to go hammering on the door of the nearest employer
and beg to be taken in. Not so Alan. He is not a great one
for hammering upon employers' doors. However, to please
me, he came with me to find work after we had been a month
at Hafod. As we left our jobs in Bristol voluntarily we were
not entitled to unemployment pay, and our bit of capital was
dwindling.

Down in the valley, about a half an hour's cycle ride away,
there was a flour mill with a small labour force. We went
there to offer our services, and were taken on. This was our
first contact with the Welsh worker. We learned how to tell
Welsh jokes, how to swear in Welsh and how to sing 'Land
of my Fathers' in Welsh. We also learned how to pack flour.

As a flour packer Alan was a dismal failure. A 3-lb bag of
flour packed by him resembled a loosely filled, badly plumped
pillow. It came in any sort of shape, but roughly spherical,

clumsily folded at the top, and with inches and inches of Sellotape plastered hopefully around it. To pack one bag took him about ten minutes. On the other hand, I soon mastered the job. With swiftly moving fingers I was able to produce a solid, symmetrical rectangular bag of flour, neatly finished with about an inch of Sellotape, in about three minutes. Alan was supposed to be making himself useful inside and outside the mill so, fortunately for the rest of us, he was only fumbling about in the flour-packing room during bad weather. He was obviously of much more use outside. But the job lasted only five months. There was some trouble over the erection of a fence. A difference of opinion between Alan and the boss. Voices were raised, strong language was used—and Alan got the sack. In rural Wales you can't swear at your employer and get away with it.

But although we were now without a job (I felt obliged to make a dignified exit from the mill at the same time) the fact that Alan had been sacked meant that he was now entitled to unemployment pay. Having been a dutiful contributor to the National Insurance scheme for many years, he claimed his benefit without a qualm and hoped that the Labour Exchange wouldn't find him a job for a couple of weeks as there was a lot of work to be done at Hafod, and a period of unemployment with pay would come in very useful. He needn't have worried. As the weeks slipped by, and then the months, it became obvious that there wasn't the remotest chance of the Labour Exchange producing a job for him. In the meantime we were both looking out for work. The newspaper was combed each week, and letters sent off when anything remotely likely was advertised in the area. Neither of us was ever called for interview. Alan went after an assembly job in a thermo-plastics factory, was interviewed by the head postmaster at Llanrwst in respect of a vacancy for a postman, and also applied to the county council for work on the roads. In each case he was told that he would be put on a waiting list. (So far as he knows he is still on these lists; he has never heard anything further about any of them.) He *was* offered one job. We were visited by a wealthy gentleman who keeps a local show house that is open to the public. He offered Alan a job repairing antique furniture, wall building, gardening and occasionally helping with coach parties. He was to start work each day at 8.0 a.m. and stay until the last coach party had left at dusk. (This would be around 9.30 p.m. during high summer.) The pay was £1 per day. Alan showed him the door. The man was quite unperturbed; he wasn't short of staff. Old-age pensioners and students were apparently happy to work for him at £1 a day.

My efforts to find work were equally unsuccessful. Having failed to discover any nearby establishment that wanted a typist, I called at the Labour Exchange in Llanrwst to ask if they thought there was any scope for me to take in typing, and work at home. I explained to the lady behind the counter that, for example, in Bristol the University farmed out work to outside typists. Was there any establishment locally that did this? With a freezingly thin smile, in which I could almost hear the ice crackle, she suggested that perhaps I had better write to Bristol University then.

This 'English-go-home' attitude is typical, in our experience, of the local government officials. It is, perhaps, understandable. In an area of low employment opportunity where there is a queue of Welshmen available for every vacant job, why should an alien intruder get any consideration?

In order to claim his unemployment pay Alan had to perform a strange weekly ritual. As we lived more than five miles from the Labour Exchange it was not necessary for him to report there each week, but he had to get someone to sign a form declaring that it was within their knowledge that Alan had not been employed by anyone in the preceding week. As we were not known locally, and no one lived near enough to know what he was up to each day, there was no one in the area who could truthfully sign such a declaration. Fortunately Alan discovered another unemployed man in a similar predicament who lived not too far away. Every Thursday they would walk to an agreed meeting point and sign each other's form. The forms were never queried.

And then he ran out of Benefit. One week he received a

notice warning him that in a week's time he would be entitled to no more unemployment pay. The time had come to look further afield for work.

It was the end of August, and too late to consider applying for work at a Holiday Camp. We considered hop picking, but decided that this would not bring us in enough money. (When Alan once tried hop picking he finished up out of pocket as some of his camping equipment was stolen.) Anyway, we really wanted something that would last the winter. If we both worked full-time for the next four or five months we should be able to make enough money to take us through the following spring and summer at Hafod.

One day I was browsing through a copy of the magazine *The Lady* that someone had given me. I started looking idly at the domestic vacancies at the back. There were page after page of them. All over the country, apparently, there were wealthy people in desperate need of housekeepers, cooks, nannies, butlers, gardeners and handymen. Here was one field of employment where it was most certainly a seller's market. Suddenly I had an idea. Might there be scope for the two of us to operate as stand-in domestic relief for a few weeks to households that were in temporary difficulties through loss of staff? We could, say, offer our services for any period of time up to five weeks, and have five weeks away earning money, then, say, a couple of weeks back at Hafod to catch up on the gardening and house repairs, followed by another four or five weeks away, and so on. Neither of us had any experience of domestic service, but we reckoned (quite correctly as it turned out) that a pair of inexperienced hands was better than no hands at all to someone who needed domestic help.

According to the advertisements in *The Lady*, an experienced domestic couple could command a joint salary of £30 a week, plus full board and perks. (This was in the late 1960s.) We decided to offer our services at a joint wage of £20 a week, plus full board (and no perks). We would operate as a self-employed team and, at the end of a five-week stint of work, we would collect payment of £100. This would be more than enough to keep us at Hafod for two months, even allowing for travelling expenses and stamping Alan's card.

We could advertise in *The Lady*, but how should we describe ourselves? What, in fact, were we prepared to do? Alan settled for the title of 'Gardener/Handyman'—which was fair enough. Plenty of them were wanted. I wasn't so easily classified. Most of the situations vacant were for cooks and nannies. I would find professional cooking a nerve-wracking worry, and I do not get on with children, although I was prepared to 'help out' with both duties. In other words I didn't mind being the cook's kitchen maid, or the nanny's assistant. I would, however, much prefer to take on the job of house cleaning or looking after domestic animals. 'General Helps' were wanted, and also 'Housemaids' but I wasn't sure what either job involved. Fortunately I had two books of reference on the subject. Both were cookery books (published, admittedly, at the turn of the century) and both contained a servants' Code of Practice at the back. I consulted first of all *The Economical Housewife*, published by Lever Bros. Ltd. Under the chapter headed 'Our Household Helps' the first help to be listed was the charwoman.

> The Charwoman—I read—we have tried and found to be a failure. She is expensive now-a-days as to her charges per week or per day—the shilling she was wont to be satisfied with in olden times will not now appease her pecuniary desires for the few short hours she makes do duty for a day, and ere she closes her bargaining with you, she will as a rule stand out valiantly for her 'drop o gin'. There *are* respectable, honest, hardworking women of their class about, of course, but they are certainly few and far between.

If I was going to get anywhere in the world below-stairs I must obviously not describe myself as a charwoman. The housemaid, on the other hand, was a much nicer sort of person:

> A thorough, well-up-to-her-business upper housemaid can be a very pillar of help to her mistress. As she is often required to wait at table, she should be rather tall, and what is called 'genteel', pleasant-faced, pleasant-mannered, and pleasant-voiced. . . .

I could probably manage the pleasant manner and pleasant voice, but I wasn't too sure about this 'genteel' bit. However, *The Economical Housewife* held out hopes for types like me:

These attributes she will speedily acquire—it went on— even if she has not them in a large degree when she comes to you first. Her path lies very much amongst her superiors. Her time is necessarily spent where the 'upstairs people' are, than in the kitchen, and so, unconsciously to herself, she will copy nicer behaviour, gentler ways than those she has been accustomed to.

On the other hand it all sounded rather snooty. I think I'd be more at home pigging it in the kitchen with the rougher mob below.

I couldn't find any information on a General Help, although in my other book (a battered, coverless family heirloom) there was a breezy paragraph on the 'General Servant'. I read it with mounting concern. Leaping out of bed at crack of dawn with a happy expression upon her Jesus-loves-me, honest working-class face, the little General Servant must throw open the shutters, dash down to the kitchen, rake out the ashes, light the range, clean and polish it, then put the kettle to boil. Running lightly then to the breakfast room, she must clean the grate, light the fire, dust and polish the room and lay the table. With never a thought for her rumbling tummy, she must then sweep the hall, shake the mats, scrub the front step, polish the knocker, and clean The Family's shoes. Now she must wash her hands and face, put on a clean apron and prepare the toast, eggs, bacon, kidneys and kippers for The Family who, by now, will be down and demanding to be fed. The tea urn and the breakfast must be carried in. Can she now retreat to the kitchen and eat her bread and scrape? Can she hell! There are the beds to strip, the windows to open and the clothes to tidy. And, before she has finished upstairs, the bell will be ringing for her to clear away the breakfast things. So, cheerfully singing a verse of 'There is a Happy Land', she will run to obey, remembering to take a brush and crumb tray, and her duster and polishing rag. For the room must be tidied, the fire made up and the hearth swept clean. 'She may then', said the book, 'have her own breakfast.'

I made a mental note *not* to describe myself as a 'General Help'.

In the end we settled for a vaguely worded advertisement simply offering our joint services; we would thrash out what we were prepared to do with whoever sought our help.

I have always responded with enthusiasm to any new idea in our personal affairs. The current plan of action occupies my thoughts to the exclusion of almost everything else, and the anticipated venture into the world of domestic service was no exception. If I was to be a servant, I wanted to be a good servant. I wanted to be a 'treasure' and bring comfort and helping hands to someone in need. I wanted to be hardworking and thoroughly dependable. Above all, I wanted always to do the Right Thing. I sought guidance from my books of reference. *The Economical Housewife* was a fund of information. I read eagerly the instructions for the care of glass, cutlery, electroplate and linen. I 'genned up' on preparing afternoon tea, the procedure for serving up dishes, and the correct way to lay the dinner table. (It is a pity that I didn't study this more carefully. I was to make a few gaffes in this quarter.) I learned that half a packet of Hudson's extract of soap was the stuff to clean your Venetian blinds (applied with a quarter-yard square of flannel) and also your bedsteads. I gathered, however, that Hudson's extract of soap wasn't up to coping with the 'bed pests' that one was likely to meet. 'Every joint must be examined and, as prevention is fifty times better than cure, well saturated or sponged with paraffin.'

I thought that perhaps the paragraph entitled 'Demeanour towards Servants' might help me to establish the correct working relationship with my future mistresses.

Education—I read—does much for the servant class now-a-days. Some say much more than it ought to do, but education such as they get, albeit it is what is termed good English, writing and a glimmering of arithmetic, does not give them one iota of *refinement*, their daily, hourly associations prevent this, and although a maid may actually spell more correctly than her mistress, there is a very wide gulf that parts these two.

Alas; it seemed that even with the 'genteel' influence of the Upstairs World of the housemaid, I was never going to be able to approach my employers on anything like equal terms. *The Economical Housewife* had a stern word of caution to the mistress on this subject:

We must not expect to find our kind, where our kind is not.

They were, however, encouraged to be generous to the poor. Like giving them the uneatable crusts:

The uneatable crusts. What are we to do with them? Soak them in two or three waters, which will be very little trouble—beat them into a pap with a few pennyworth of sugar (sugar is so cheap now) a few currants or not, as you choose, put this with a little dripping into a pan, bake, and gladden the hearts of somebody's hungry little ones with the timely, inexpensive, thoughtful gift.

Stale dripping was recommended for a similar worthy cause:

Stale dripping. It must be very bad indeed if it cannot be clarified and made fit for *something*. If once pouring boiling water upon it does not have the desired effect, do it two or three times. Pieces of bread collected from the dinner table, or left over from the nursery can then be soaked in it to make a bread pudding.

If nobody's 'hungry little ones' could be found as recipient of your bread pudding, you were advised to give it to your servants, 'but'—the paragraph continued in a puzzled tone—

servants are sometimes strenuously averse to eating what they term 'leavings', especially children's leavings.

This book was published at the end of the last century. I was to find that things haven't changed much in the world of domestic service.

We had one immediate response to our advertisement. On headed notepaper, it was signed by a 'Personal Secretary' on behalf of her employer, requesting our services immediately at the family home in Sussex. I was appalled. Her employer was a well-known figure; a *very* well-known figure—who moved in a social circle far above that of *The Economical Housewife*. I had been hoping that we would be taken on by some elderly and grateful clergyman, or retired army officer's widow or somesuch. We wrote back at once expressing our willingness to help out but listing all the reasons why we were so obviously unsuitable for such an appointment—even a temporary one. A reply from the 'Personal Secretary' came by return of post. Our inexperience did not matter, and would we please report to the Hon. Mrs. Tubbland-Tipper (that is not her real name of course) as soon as possible. There was nothing for it but to oblige. We secured everything at Hafod, locked the front gate, and drove to Sussex.

It was a worrying drive. Alan was silent most of the time. His duties had been specified as chauffeur/valet/gardener/handyman, which struck me as being a rather odd combination. However, Alan made the reasonable assumption that, as he was supposed to be able to do *all* of them, he could not be expected to do any of them very well. He reckoned that his experience as a batman would help him over the valet part, and there were no fears of his abilities as a handyman. He could drive, so presumably he could 'chauffeur' but I was not too sure of his ability to give satisfaction as a gardener. Would the Hon. Mrs. Tubbland-Tipper *mind* about the patches of nettles he would insist upon leaving for the larvae of the peacock butterflies, and the 'interesting' weeds he would wish to preserve in her flower borders? I foresaw trouble.

I had two surprises when we got there. First of all 'The Grange' was not the rambling Victorian house I had expected, but an unimpressive modern building. (There *had* been a rambling Victorian house there but it was burnt down three years ago owing, apparently, to Mrs. Tubbland-Tipper's faulty electric blanket.) Mrs. Tubbland-Tipper herself, aged about twenty-nine, bare-footed, beaded and wearing a sarong, was the second shock. Apparently this was not the household of THE Tubbland-Tippers, but that of his son. To be working for people who were younger than us struck me as being very odd. For some reason I had always imagined us working for the sick or the elderly. It never entered my head that people who were young and healthy would want servants. However, as Mrs. Tubbland-Tipper took us on a conducted tour of her house, I could see why she was so desperate for help. Toys and magazines were scattered everywhere; there was dust on all surfaces, bits of cotton, fluff and mud on the carpets, and two piles of dog's mess in one of the bedrooms.

My duties were vaguely defined. I was supposed to make myself generally useful in the house. This was all very well, but my usefulness was somewhat impaired by the lack of suitable cleaning equipment. There was a distinctly dodgy vacuum cleaner, and one sweeping brush, but no dust-pan—so I had to make do with the coal shovel. There were no decent rags or dusters. Instead I was supplied with a pillow-case filled with Mrs. Tubbland-Tipper's cast-off nylon underwear and old cardigans, complete with buttons. And there was no soap in the kitchen. Packets and packets of detergent powder, but no soap. You would never realize how many times a day you pick up the soap to wash your hands, until you work in a kitchen that hasn't any.

My first job of the day was to wash up the breakfast things and the dinner things from the previous night. Each morning there was congealed gravy, or crusted layers of burnt vegetables, fish or porridge to be removed from the mountain of pots and pans—but there was no pan cleaner. There was, however, a massive dishwashing machine that gurgled and thumped impressively and produced cups, saucers and cutlery that were sparkling with an even coat of detergent. Closer examination revealed that circulating bits of meat, vegetables and egg had been securely glazed to the gleaming surfaces of cups and plates alike. However, one morning a couple of days after I had taken charge this gleaming monster gave a deep-throated gurgle over the breakfast dishes, growled wearily, belched, and then shuddered to a halt. Alan refused to look at it, and the thing lay immobile and useless for the rest of our stay. In the meantime I persuaded Mrs. Tubbland-

Tipper to let me buy a dishcloth and pan-cleaner, and from then on the washing up was done in a civilized manner.

Permanent staff kept at The Grange were a groom, a head gardener and a nanny. There should also have been a cook but there was not one at the moment and Nanny, with much grumbling, was standing in. She had been there for only three months, and was leaving next month. There was one child in the household. Amelia Tubbland-Tipper was eight years old, shrill and sulky. Nanny got her up each morning and gave her breakfast. She was taken to school by the current chauffeur, and collected by him in the afternoon. Nanny then gave her tea, and she spent the evening in the nursery (if it was wet) or out in the grounds or visiting other children with Nanny (if it was fine). She broke her toys, screamed at her Nanny and kicked doors, furniture and dogs. She had a pony, a heated swimming pool and a nursery full of large toys, including her own television set. In fact she had plenty of everything—except affection. During our five weeks' stay I didn't see anyone kiss or cuddle her.

The only thoroughly reliable member of the household appeared to be Barkshaw. He looked after the gardens, fed the chickens, and came in every morning to refuel the Aga. He was a Sussex man and had always been in service—for the past thirty years with the Tubbland-Tippers, (senior and then junior). 'Gentry?' he said to me one morning over our cup of coffee, 'I've worked for 'em all me life,' and he hawked juicily into the coal hod.

Alan's combination of duties meant that he was continually changing his clothes. He wore overalls for cleaning the cars and attending to repair jobs in the house (and there were plenty of those—nothing worked properly), and old clothes and wellington boots when helping Barkshaw in the garden. But twice a day he had to put on a tidy suit to act as chauffeur to Miss Amelia, and sometimes again in mid-morning if Mrs. Tubbland-Tipper wanted him to take her shopping. His duties as valet were confined to packing Mr. Tubbland-Tipper's case when he went off for a trip, and unpacking the dirty clothes when he returned.

As Mr. Tubbland-Tipper had never learned to drive (and

seemed to have a fear of cars) he used to travel mostly by train. Chauffeuring him between home and the station was another of Alan's regular duties.

At the end of our agreed five weeks' tour of duty Mrs. Tubbland-Tipper asked if we would stay on. The new nanny had just arrived, but there was apparently no other 'help' in the offing. When we regretfully declined she just shrugged her shoulders and strolled back to the house. And, presumably, the dirty crocks, the fluff, litter and dog's mess started to pile up again as we drove away.

13. EARNING MORE MONEY

There was a stack of post waiting for us at Hafod. People were writing from all over the country, asking us to go and work for them. We would obviously be able to pick and choose. It was now October, and there was a lot to be done in the garden. Half a dozen marrows had ripened in our absence, and also the Japanese wineberries. There were a lot of peas left, and these would have to be picked and dried. Grass and weeds were growing lushly everywhere. The weather was warm and calm. We worked outside steadily for a fortnight whilst we discussed our next move.

We decided to arrange a programme of work that would take us through to the end of March, allowing a fortnight in between each job for us to return to check up on things at Hafod. We should then have made enough money to enable us to enjoy the summer at Hafod without worrying about earning a living.

During the next few months we became stand-in servants to wealthy households in Berkshire, Surrey, Cheshire, Shropshire, Oxfordshire and Herefordshire. I always tried to remain amongst the lower orders in the household, but was invariably called upon to stand in for nanny and also to cook. Laying the dinner table was always a bit of an ordeal. I could never be sure that I had not forgotten something, and it was a great help if Alan came behind me. 'Will you never learn?' he would cry in despair as he reversed the cutlery, rearranged glasses and napkins and repositioned condiments, 'This is the Manor House—not a bloody Youth Hostel!' But I received only one complaint from the mistress. 'Elizabeth, I think we have a little silver jug that would look rather better than this,' and, with a charming smile, she handed me the saucer containing a carton of cream with a teaspoon stuck in it that I had plonked on the dinner table.

Generally speaking we found that my services were more urgently required than Alan's. Consequently he had a much easier time of it. Whilst I laboured from dawn to dusk in the house, he would disappear for hours on end 'helping the gardener'—which often meant squatting down behind some sunny wall, or sitting in the greenhouse, exchanging tobacco and yarns.

Our last engagement was at a crumbling Baronial Hall in Derbyshire. From the lodge gates to the Hall itself was a half-mile drive through parkland and around a vast lake, ringed with reedmace and scuttling with coot and moorhen.

Each morning I drew back the curtains at the Hall and gazed out over the lake. It was always wrapped in early morning mist which lifted slowly in the weak March sunshine, and slid away in long fingers between the trees. The view from those tall windows had changed little in the last hundred years and it was possible, in those first few minutes, to catch the feeling of England at the turn of the century. The countryside secure, timeless and middle class; peacocks on the lawn, carriages at the door, and all's well with the empire.

But the dream faded with the lifting of the mist. This was 1968 and nothing was secure any more. Rank dead grass sprouted in tufts between the paving stones on the terrace, balustrades were crumbling, and facing slabs were falling off the front of the house. The ornate game-larder, the stables and coach house were in ruins. The roof of one wing of the house was falling in, and some chimney pots were leaning dangerously.

Sir Ernest and Lady Lilian Hartlingthorpe were in their late seventies. The last of a long line of Hartlingthorpes of the Hall, they were the only people we had served who were of the upper class. They were also the poorest.

Lady Lilian stood an erect 4 feet 10 inches, very thin, with short-cropped grey hair, a large bony nose, hard blue eyes and a severe expression. Her manner was composed, aggressively self-assured and absolutely domineering. Our relationship of mistress and servant was established instantly and smoothly. I found myself calling her 'Ma'am' quite naturally and without the slightest hesitation. Her Demeanour towards Servants was straight out of *The Economical Housewife*. I would not mind betting she had a copy of it somewhere. She knew exactly the correct way to deal with footman, butler, parlour-maid, chambermaid, cook and kitchen staff. Unfortunately, she could not afford any of them. She had to make do with Alan and me. There was one 'outside staff' called Henderson; the ubiquitous faithful old-timer who looked after a patch of garden, fed the chickens and came in to stoke up the Aga. But this one was rather silent and surly. He did not want to know us, and certainly did not want Alan 'poking around and interfering' in his garden. So Alan kept out of his way and helped me in the Hall.

My day started at 7.30 a.m. when I took up a tray of breakfast to Lady Lilian. At 8.15 a.m. I went to collect it from her. I took with me a notepad and pencil, because she would wish to discuss with me the menus for the day. Lapsing into nineteenth-century nostalgia, she would sometimes toy with the idea of having baked sturgeon and mussels, served with braised celery cream and mushrooms St. Honoré. Or possibly a pie. Perhaps we should have rumpsteak and oyster pie, or devilled game, served with fregarhed greens and kidney beans fricasseed. But she always came back to a tin of stewed steak, carrots and roast potatoes followed by rice pudding; or macaroni cheese and apple crumble. The instructions were given, and received, with dignity.

Sir Ernest was tall, very thin, given to wearing plus-fours, and looked very much like George Bernard Shaw. He preferred to eat alone, and frugally, in a small breakfast room alongside the kitchen. (No doubt because it was the warmest room in the house, apart from the kitchen.) He was an aloof man and rarely spoke to us. He always carried with him a small portable radio, which seemed oddly out of character, but the only programme I ever heard him listening to was *The Archers*.

The whole place was falling to bits. Alan did a quick lash-up repair of the bell system, so that Lady Lilian could now ring for us from any room in the house. (I think that this repair job gave her more pleasure than anything else we did for her.) He also repaired floorboards, replaced a few of the broken window panes, and crawled out onto the roof to try and stop some of the leaks. He did an expert repair and restoration job on a seventeenth-century oak chest he found in an attic room. He was not asked to do this; he did it because he felt that it ought to be done. The box was damaged and encrusted with the dirt of centuries, but it was basically of sound construction and pleasing design. Out of respect for the hands that made it (and not for the benefit of the people who owned it) Alan took great care, working with chisel, gouge, spokeshave, cabinet scrape and shellac. The result was a box that was now both functional and beautiful. He returned it to the attic quite unconcerned that, in all probability, his work would go unnoticed. In fact he prided himself that it would take an expert to detect that the box had been broken. He had established a cordial link of brotherhood across the centuries with the man who had made the box. That was his satisfaction.

The glorious past of the Hartlingthorpes hung sadly and dustily all around us. There was a large library on the first floor (never entered because the floor was unsafe), a large and gloomy portrait gallery, and an entrance hall hung with faded tattered banners and stags' heads. The smell of decay was everywhere. We were almost too nervous to touch things, in case they should crumble to dust in front of us. There was only one accident. Late in the afternoon one day Lady Lilian rang for me to come and draw the curtains. I did not, at the time, appreciate the traditional importance of this little ritual. Always eager to please, I strode across the drawing room to the tall windows where the heavy tapestries hung from ceiling to floor. I set about the job of drawing curtains in the way I was used to. Catching hold of the side of one curtain I gave it a hefty yank. There was a faint purring sound as the fabric ripped; a mere whispering sigh as the elderly threads parted company ... and I stood there with a ragged square foot of cloth in my hand. The expression upon my face must have looked like something out of an early *Punch* cartoon as I turned to face Her Ladyship, 'Oh—er Mum, it came orf in me 'and!' Lady Lilian rose with a sigh. 'Perhaps *I* had better draw them Elizabeth.'

Her attitude to me was always one of controlled patience. She was never angry, but I never saw her pleased either. In fact she displayed no emotions whatsoever. She never laughed, raised her voice, exchanged small talk or was the slightest bit familiar. She was remote and imperial. She only spoke to me to give instructions—and these came about every half-hour throughout the day. Not only was she constantly wanting trays of tea, she would also ring for me to pass her a magazine that was at the other side of the room, or to place another log on the fire. I obeyed meekly and with no feelings of resentment. Sometimes she came down to the kitchen to go through the stocks. She did this on our first day there, and opening a cake tin she found a wedge of very old and mildewy jam sponge. She poked it about with a none-too-clean forefinger, then lifted it from the tin and handed it to me. 'I think that this is rather stale,' she said loftily, 'perhaps you and Alan would like it.' I thanked her humbly, and put it out for the birds as soon as she had gone. It was impossible to feel offended. She lived honestly by the only code she knew. Servants were inferior but necessary parts of one's household—like the dogs. One treated them in a kind but firm manner, and occasionally threw them scraps. If one was patient with them they were loyal and obedient.

During the five weeks we were at the Hall the Hartling-thorpes received only two visitors; a couple of men who called together to enquire about the shooting rental of the parkland. As it was obvious to us that the front door was never used, we guessed when we heard the knocking that strangers were without. We were both standing in the entrance hall at the time. Alan was reglazing an inner door, and I had just brought him a cup of tea. Alan went immediately to draw the bolts on the door, and I picked up his cup of tea and stood back to hide in a gloomy banner-shrouded corner.

Alan will always rise to an occasion—and his performance at the front door that afternoon would have gained top marks from *The Economical Housewife*. Having ascertained the business of the callers, he invited them in with just the hint of a dignified bow, and a slight gesture of his right arm. He stated his intention of taking them to the drawing room whilst he made enquiries to see if Sir Ernest was At Home. 'May I take your coats, gentlemen?' he said with English-country-house-butler's diction straight out of Wodehouse. The two men stepped inside and dutifully took off their coats. They were obviously ill at ease. One man tugged at his collar and looked around apprehensively as the great door was closed behind him. The other one kept clearing his throat. Alan juggled with the coats for a moment. It was quite obvious to me that, having taken them, he hadn't the remotest idea what to do with them. He cast an eye towards a dusty pair of antlers hanging nearby, thought better of it, and rearranged the coats across his arm. 'Perhaps you will come this way, gentlemen,' he said haughtily, stepping forward with a dignified measured tread. As stand-in butler for the Hartlingthorpes he was certainly doing his stuff. He recognized an inferior class of person when he saw one, and he was certainly putting these men in their place. They shuffled behind him across the hall. But when he switched on the corridor lights their eyes bulged in amazement. I don't think that it was the gaunt dusty hall that took them aback so much as the appearance of the 'butler', whose lofty manner was somewhat offset by the paint-daubed corduroy trousers, unravelling old Harris pullover and shabby carpet slippers that he was wearing.

On reflection I think that perhaps the whole episode was entirely in keeping with the Mad-Hatter's Tea Party atmosphere of the place. Sir Ernest refused to see the men, and told Alan to refer them to his agent. Lady Lilian was ringing bells for me all the time they were in the house, and on the way out one of them put his foot through a rotten floorboard. They finally escaped in their Mini, having stalled it twice in their agitated eagerness to get away.

One day during our last week at the Hall, Lady Lilian asked us both to attend her in the drawing room. She then settled up with us, and gave us each £1 extra as a 'bonus', and thanked us graciously for looking after them so well. I was genuinely touched. She asked us if we would consider staying with them longer. We refused—as gently as possible.

Until then I had not stopped to wonder how they would manage once we had left. It was obvious (and understandable) that she would have difficulty in getting the sort of household help she wanted. And, so far as I was aware, Lady Lilian was incapable of doing the simplest task in the kitchen. She certainly did not understand how the Aga worked for a start. The dilemma was one that the Hartlingthorpes had obviously faced before, and they knew what they would have to do. On our last day there I was asked to pack up their suitcases, and Alan was to drive them to a hotel about fifteen miles away. We were to close the shutters at the Hall that same evening, turn off the water and electricity, and lock up—handing the key in to Henderson at the gatehouse as we left.

I packed up four suitcases as instructed, and helped Alan carry them down to the car. The Hartlingthorpes came out carrying rugs, a small leather holdall and, of course, the portable radio. Alan stowed everything into the boot and held open the door of the car. As I said good-bye to Lady Lilian the change in our relationship was already taking place. The cloak of Imperial Power was slipping away from her shoulders like a worn-out old shawl. For five weeks now we had acted our parts; she the mistress, I the servant. But now the play was over. The final curtain had dropped, and the actors were resuming their normal roles. She was no longer Lady Lilian of the Hall, but a rather tired old woman being shuffled about by ill fortune. Sir Ernest took one last dejected look around at the lake and the woods before clambering into the car. They could have been a couple of old mumpers being carted off to the Salvation Army hostel.

14. LOSING MONEY

'We must think of a profitable sideline,' Alan said one day. It had been a good summer. We had not been urgently looking for work and yet, in the contrary manner of fate, the odd bit of casual employment came our way. But I agreed that it would be a good idea to have a sideline. Everyone had sidelines. Some farmers did bed and breakfast and ran caravan sites, the grocer drove the school bus, the council lengthman dealt in scrap iron, and the postman kept a pig.

The keeping of animals appeared to be the obvious sideline for us. According to the postman, vast fortunes could be made out of pigs and, with our outbuildings and bit of land, it seemed that we couldn't go wrong. It was quite common, apparently, for a sow to have a litter of fourteen or fifteen young and—going by the postman's figures—Alan reckoned that four sows could give us a good basic income. So we bought a book on pig-keeping. And then had second thoughts.

My pleasant pastoral picture of mother sow grazing happily with her piglets around the scrubby hillside faded when faced with the cold facts of pig-keeping. Although pigs did indeed have large litters you were liable to lose the lot through (a) pneumonia, (b) mother rolling on them, or (c) mother eating them. And it was sometimes necessary to keep mother pinned to the ground by a wooden crate during the latter part of her 'confinement' in order to prevent her maltreating her newborn young. Scours, Mange Encrustation and The Trembles were nasty ailments lying in wait for young pigs, and it was recommended that you got cracking with a hypodermic syringe, some 1 inch long 'stout needles' and an assortment of serums from the word go. Then there was castration. This had to be done when the piglets were three weeks old. One of us would have to hold piggy's legs apart whilst the other wielded the knife. We couldn't do it. Alternatively, we need not deal with a sow. We could buy young piglets that someone else had already done the dirty on, and fatten them up to the required weight for selling. But I know what would happen. We would give our pigs names, get to know each one's personality, and then not be able to take the final treacherous step of selling them to the slaughterer.

What about a cow? We could run one at Hafod, and have the benefit of her milk, plus one calf a year which we could sell. But the same thing would happen. When a calf is taken for slaughtering, the mother will bellow with grief for days. When it came to the crunch we knew that we could not bear to part Mum from her calf—so we would end up keeping cow and calf, and not getting any milk either.

It was obvious that we would never become farmers. As we still drink milk, eat a lot of cheese and occasionally some meat —this makes us a pair of hypocrites. We could probably give up eating meat (the way prices are soaring we may have to anyway) but such a sanctimonious gesture would be equally hypocritical. We shall always want to drink milk, eat butter, cheese and eggs, wear leather and wool, and use down quilts, glue and soap. Somehow or other we must come to terms with the fact that, in order for us to live in the world as it is today, some animals must die. This being so, we should have the guts to deal with the unpleasantries of farming ourselves. But we haven't. So we remain a pair of hypocrites.

Now if only we could make a living from selling eggs, that would suit us fine. I would enjoy looking after a couple of hundred hens, and could take their eggs from them without a single pang of conscience. But no matter how optimistically we try to juggle the figures the fact remains that, if you have to buy foodstuff for your hens, you will make a loss on the eggs unless you have vast flocks and a good collection system, or are on a main road and can sell direct to the public.

So we shelved the idea of making money out of animals, and considered how we could make money out of people.

Some people have a gift for making money; others have not. A person blessed with this gift will succeed whether he

147

trades in battleships or bootlaces. The merchandise does not matter; the gift is all important. Without it, any speculative enterprise is doomed. After several years of wasted effort and money we now know, beyond all doubt, that we have no such gift. Show us a business opportunity, and we will make a mess of it. Invest your capital in us, and we will lose the lot for you.

I think that the fault lies partly with our basic attitudes. We have never been genuinely whole-hearted about any scheme. We have never really *wanted* to make money, we just thought that we ought to, in order to supplement our extremely unreliable and casual wages.

Buying and selling was an early idea. When we first came to Hafod we were surprised at the number of dealers who brought their lorries grinding up the track to Hafod. Had we anything to sell? Scrap metal, junk, old furniture, crockery? They were interested in everything. We sold a couple of old car batteries to the first one that came, but after that we had nothing to sell. Hafod, with its miscellaneous stacks of timber, corrugated iron, bits of netting and ironmongery may *look* like a dealer's dream of rich pickings, but the fact is that we need most of our junk, and would not dream of parting with any item that might conceivably be of use to us at some future date. But how about attending some farm sales and buying some stuff cheaply in order to sell to the next dealer who called? It should be possible to pick up a job lot that contained all sorts of junk that a dealer might be interested in.

Crockery seemed the best bet. The traditional willow-pattern service that adorns many Welsh dressers seemed to be always in demand, so we set out one day to attend a farm sale for the purely mercenary reason of making some money. We kept a careful note of what we spent (including petrol and an allowance for wear and tear on the vehicle) and reckoned that £20 covered the total cost of the expedition. We came back with a goodly load of willow-pattern meat dishes, glassware, jug and basin sets and some 'fairground' vases. We stored them in the shippen, and waited for the next dealer to call. And we are still waiting. Not a single dealer has called at Hafod since then.

Our next misadventure was a much bigger one. It cost us about £245, much wasted effort and a lot of worry.

We decided to buy a caravan. Tourism is one of the main sources of income in North Wales, and we reckoned that the only way in which we could cash in on it was by offering a furnished caravan for rent during the summer. A level site could be made for it in the field, it would be well screened by the hawthorn hedge, and whoever rented it could be sure of peace and solitude. They would have to settle for spring water and a chemical closet, but we could fix up the caravan with electric light from Charlie. Cooking and heating would be by bottled gas. Certainly such primitive solitude would only appeal to a few people—but then, we only wanted a few people. It was never our intention to have more than one caravan. The more we thought about it, the more enthusiastic we became. We could make it a very comfortable caravan. We could put up illustrations of the bird and animal life likely to be seen in the area. We could suggest walks, lend maps, perhaps even sell people fruit and vegetables from the garden. We could imagine it becoming a highly satisfying experience, with the same contented customers coming back year after year to stay at Hafod. So we bought a caravan.

It was a second-hand 27 foot Pemberton, and we employed an expert with a Land-Rover and winch to collect it and get it up the track and into the Hafod field. After much difficulty (and a broken winch) it was finally there, on its intended site behind the hawthorn hedge, and Alan got to work on it. The caravan was supposed to accommodate six people, but when all the beds were down there was not much room for anyone to move around. What's more, it was all rather scruffy. Alan decided to de-gut it completely and rebuild it as a four-berth caravan. All the units were taken to pieces and stacked away in the stable; the cushions and bedding came into the cottage.

One day Alan was out in the field peacefully working upon the caravan when he noticed a man climbing over the gate. As the man strode across to him Alan could see that his manner was somewhat aggressive. At the first words of 'Welsh or English?' Alan assumed that a local extremist was about to attack him, and he picked up a spanner in self-defence. In view of what subsequently happened he wishes fervently that he had not waited for further explanation of the intrusion, but waded straight in with his spanner. But he didn't. He let the man state his business, and his business, it seemed, was official. He was from the local council.

In the ensuing conversation Alan gathered that by having a caravan upon his land he had broken some law. From the man's attitude it seemed that he was taking this infringement as a personal affront, and Alan's request for him to clear off and mind his own business cannot have improved his temper. He went declaring that we should hear more of this. We did. A couple of weeks later a sheaf of documents arrived from the county headquarters, including a long formal looking paper starting with the word WHEREAS. It was an enforcement order stating that if we did not move the caravan from its site within twenty-eight days we should be fined £100 and a further £20 for each day that the caravan remained there. We had, apparently, run foul of the Town and Country Planning Act.

It was necessary, we learned, to have planning permission before one could place a caravan upon one's land; that is to say, if it was a caravan like ours. If it was a motorized caravan, planning permission was not required, and one could park a 'box trailer' where one wanted without permission. So what constituted a 'caravan'? Ours was completely denuded of all fittings. If we put a horse in it would it become a horse-box? If we put chickens in it would it become a chicken-house? The council would not be drawn into such arguments. What we had done constituted a breach of planning control. And the days of the Enforcement Order were ticking by. So we wrote back applying for planning permission and apologizing for our unwitting infringement, and explaining our intentions. Planning permission was refused. We were in an area of 'great landscape value' they said, and our caravan tucked behind the hedge constituted a 'development'. The Planning Refusal went on: 'The development is out of character with its surroundings, it is detrimental to the amenity of the area and conflicts with the policy of the Local Planning Authority which seeks to preserve and enhance the natural beauty of the area.' High and mighty sentiments indeed. But what did they actually mean? When we asked a visiting official where on our ground we *could* put the caravan without infringing the law he said it could go anywhere within the curtilage of the house, i.e. within the garden fence. The only place within the garden fence where we thought that it was physically possible to get the caravan was about thirty yards away from the house up the hill, where it had no concealment whatsoever. So what it boiled down to was that by keeping a caravan neatly concealed behind a hawthorn hedge we were guilty of breaking the law and liable to a £100 fine, but by keeping a caravan half-way up a hill exposed to a vast stretch of countryside from Ffestiniog to Moel Siabod we were conforming to the Planner's policy of preservation and enhancement of the natural beauty of the area.

We sent a Notice of Appeal to the Welsh Office. This meant that the Enforcement Order would go on ice for the time being, and it gave us a few months' breathing space. We wriggled around for other loopholes. The Enforcement Order claimed that having a caravan in the field constituted a 'material change of use of the land'. We hastened to assure the council that the use of the land had not, and would not, change as a result of the caravan being there. It was, and would always be, rough grazing for sheep. The only bit of land where the sheep could not graze would be where the wheels rested, and we were perfectly willing to move the caravan occasionally to allow this bit to be grazed. The council were not interested. They were preparing their case against us, and they sent us a copy of their statement and plan. This gave us another time-winning idea. If we could shift the caravan a few yards so that it no longer conformed to the 'X' shown on their plan—and then notified them that we had moved the caravan from the position complained of in the Enforcement Order—this would mean more official visits, more pronouncements that the new site also constituted a 'breach of planning control'. A new plan would have to be produced and a new Enforcement Order made. At the rate at which councils normally work, we reckoned on gaining a few more months.

The arguments and the correspondence went on. In the end we managed to gain a reprieve for three years. But there was no question of us ever getting permission to keep the caravan in the field for a longer period.

With the local authority temporarily off our backs we sat down to consider what to do with the caravan. In its present de-gutted state there did not seem to be much chance of selling it (although one of the visiting officials hinted, with a nod and a wink, that a pal of his often helped people in difficulties with Enforcement Orders by making a quick purchase of caravans—if the price was right) so we looked again at the permitted parking area within the garden fence to see if we could find a better position for it. (The Planning Authority might be content with it being in full view upon our hillside, but we were not.) There was a neat rectangle between the stable and the cottage where it could fit quite nicely, and be almost totally concealed within the Hafod group of buildings, but we could see no way of getting it there. A large patch of bog and the spring stream and pond lay in the way, and the whole surrounding area was closely planted with our young trees. Even supposing that we could build up a roadway of sufficient strength to carry the weight of the caravan and towing vehicle, there was no room for manoeuvring once the 'convoy' had reached the site. The towing vehicle would not be able to get out! What we needed was a helicopter.

Alan sat and pondered the problem. And then came up with the answer. So simple, and so neat that I could not believe that it would work. There would be no expense of hiring an expert with Land-Rover and winch; in fact we need have no help from anyone else. We would move it ourselves; just me, Alan and a 30 bob miniature block and tackle.

To move the caravan from the field to a position between the stable and the cottage meant first of all climbing a slight hump in the field, then dropping down a steepish slope to the boggy bit. From there the ground would be dug out level for the rest of the way. The plan was this. To shift it over the hump it was more convenient to pull the caravan out backwards. So the cable would be fixed to the back of the caravan and I would pull it backwards over the tump whilst

Alan helped by levering with a crow-bar at the jockey wheel. Once over the tump the caravan would then be swung around for going down the slope. I would dig-in up the slope with my block and tackle, and pay it out bit by bit, slowly lowering the caravan down the slope, with Alan standing by with chocks. Once on the straight, the caravan would be lined up so that traversing the bog, stream and pond could be done in one straight unhesitating pull on a plain rope.

First of all Alan built up a level roadway of stone, wood and paving slabs across the bog, and strengthened and widened the causeway across the stream—laying drain-pipes where necessary. Fortunately, during the whole of the caravan moving period (it took about three weeks) the weather remained dry.

I still could not believe that the operation would work until I was actually on the pulling end of the rope, and then the sensation of moving the van was quite eerie. I was told to catch hold of the rope and run up the tump until the pulley blocks met. I did so. It felt as though I was pulling the rope through thick treacle, but when I came to the end of the run I was amazed to see that for the 20 yards I had covered, the caravan had in fact shifted—about $7\frac{1}{2}$ feet. I could see that this was not going to be a five-minute job.

As the caravan was being hauled backwards uphill, the jockey wheel frequently dug into the soft slope, so it was essential for Alan to be at that end levering with the crow-bar. It was also essential for us to work in co-ordination, and this wasn't altogether easy. We were separated by 27 feet of bulky caravan. At one point half-way up the tump the jockey wheel dug itself deeply into the soft earth and the caravan came to a full stop. 'It's going to take a mighty heave to get it out of that,' Alan said. 'Get a fresh grip on the rope, and as I start levering to take the weight off the jockey wheel, you pull for all you're worth.' I set myself up. Then, as I heard the clink of Alan's crow-bar against the jockey wheel I heaved. Nothing happened. I heaved and heaved, and my feet started slipping. I turned around, laid the rope over my shoulder and then, head down I gave the mightiest pull ever. I thought for a moment that she shifted—and then my feet went from beneath me and I was flat on my face in the grass, the rope in a heap beside me. Then Alan's voice came from behind the caravan. 'Right, I'm all set up. You can start pulling—NOW.'

Slowly, and relatively smoothly, moving a few feet at a time, the caravan was shifted from the field, and the day came when it was lined up in front of the causeway Alan had built across the bog and the stream at the point where it entered the pond. This was the tricky bit. It would be a comparatively smooth and easy pull, but if the caravan wandered a few inches to the left or right, it would be over the side and into the water. And that would be that. Once again I was on the pulling end of the rope. But this time Alan stood and supervised. I was told to pull smoothly and *fast*. This meant charging straight into a bed of nettles ahead, but now was not the time to worry about stung legs. However, I had no sooner bounded cheerfully into them when I was told to stop pulling for God's sake and come and help push it back. The causeway was, apparently, beginning to sink under the weight of the caravan. With shoulders to the caravan we pushed her back beyond the bog, and Alan spent the rest of the day strengthening the causeway. When we tried it again the following day, the caravan rolled over the bog, stream and pond without any hesitation. Another day's manœuvring amongst the nettles and she was there—sitting squat in the neat dug-out rectangle between stable and cottage.

But what of our plan to rent it out? That was now out of the question. To have visitors holidaymaking a few feet from the back door would not be a happy state of affairs for either them or us. And anyway, the whole idea had gone sour on us. It had caused us a lot of trouble and worry, and we were now only too glad to be able to forget about it. We extended our tree plantation to surround it completely and now, five years later, it is almost buried from view amongst the evergreen foliage. It is not completely useless because, being quite vermin-free, it is an ideal place to store our winter vegetables. It is much better than a clamp, but then—at £245—it ought to be!

The Authorities had not entirely finished with us. The District Valuer was next on the scene to check whether or not we were using the caravan as a spare bedroom, because if we were we would then have to pay rates on it. He looked at the caravan, the surrounding trees, the pond, stream and bog, and he was obviously puzzled as to how we got it there. 'Oh, the wife pulled it,' Alan replied offhandedly to his question. 'It's surprising what you can do with a strong wife and a bit of rope.'

The caravan fiasco has a sequel. The following year we received a circular letter that had been sent from the County Planning officer to all farms and smallholdings in the area. Headed 'Farms and Tourism Study' it enclosed a questionnaire and invited us to say whether we had ever considered catering for holidaymakers by providing caravans. If not, why not? 'You may benefit from tourism,' the letter pointed out, 'tourism can help to check depopulation and preserve the traditions of the Welsh rural community ...'

Growing Christmas trees was the next idea. According to the information we had read on the subject, one bought them as four-year-olds (nominally 12 to 18 inches high) and sold them a few years later when they reached 3 to 4 feet. We thought it sounded a good idea, so we contacted a local nurseryman and arranged for an annual supply. Every spring, for the following four years, Alan laboured away in the field with his spade planting two thousand trees. Now, six years later, we have eight thousand trees struggling to grow up there on the hill, only a few of which have made it to 4 feet. Many of them are not much bigger than when they were planted. (They now range from 9 inches to about 4 feet 6 inches.)

'The Norway spruce,' we had read, 'is frost hardy, whereas the Sitka spruce is tender.' I'd like to meet the man who wrote that. I'd like to take him by the ear and show him our plantation of Sitka spruce trees growing straight and strong, with never a sign of frost damage—and then drag him up to the plantation of Norway spruce, most of which are cowering nervously beneath the grass. Any tree rash enough to soar skywards with its leader shows the scars of its battle for survival. Some are completely devoid of branches on their windward sides, others have grown scorched needleless tips where the frost got them, and many sport half a dozen crooked leaders in the place of the one that was snapped off in a gale. And how many people want half a dozen fairies on top of their trees?

One day, hopefully, we might sell a few trees. (Last year we were offered £20 for four hundred 3 or 4 foot ones.) But it is now obvious that we shall lose money on the scheme. So what? We can shrug our shoulders at lost money. But the thought of all that wasted effort makes us wince. It wasn't only planting the things—we are still clearing the grass from around them each autumn, straightening them up when they are blown sideways, and pruning to correct frost and gale damage in the forlorn hope of encouraging some sort of Christmassy shape.

I reckon that every tree in that plantation has ten minutes of time spent upon it every year. And there are eight thousand of them up there. You work it out—and sympathize with us.

We have now given up pursuing money-making schemes. And during all the years that we were wasting time and money chasing fancy ideas, Alan was unwittingly developing a perfectly satisfactory sideline of his own—that of 'technical tinker'.

It is perhaps more accurate to say that this sideline (which has now become his main line) was thrust upon him. Whilst perfectly happy to botch, repair and fix things in his own house, he has always been somewhat chary about taking on jobs for other people. But having done one or two jobs for neighbours, his reputation as a general 'Fixit' became known, and an increasing number of people are finding their way up the track to Hafod carrying mechanical contrivances that won't work, or bringing requests to come and look at some equipment that has gone wrong. They are usually greeted with a gloomy face, a suspicious manner, and a blank denial of any specialized knowledge of anything whatsoever. They may be forgiven for thinking they have come to the wrong address, but just before they are about to depart, they are invited to leave whatever it is they have brought and Alan will warily agree to 'have a look at it'. Once their back is turned, the attitude of uninterested caution is changed to one of nimble-fingered curiosity. The thing will be in pieces before the departing customer has reached the front gate, and the chances are that it will be repaired before he has reached his home.

His method of charging is haphazard, and with friends and neighbours normally no charge is made—a system of trading service for goods being a much friendlier arrangement. If he goes off to a neighbour's house to do a job, he usually comes home carrying a hunk of meat or a dozen eggs—and everyone is happy. But this system of payment in 'kind' is full of surprises. He once spent the morning working at the house of a friend who usually pays him with a piece of lamb. Sometimes it is pork, and sometimes eggs. On this particular day, having nothing in mind for dinner that evening, I determined to make a meal out of whatever it was Alan would be bringing home. From the delighted 'guess what I've got' look on his face as he walked up the path, I thought that at least a leg of lamb or half a side of bacon was forthcoming. He produced from his rucksack 35 yards of 1.5 mm 4 core cable, and two dozen galvanized roofing bolts.

Our other source of income is casual employment. Temporary and seasonal work can often be found, now that we are known. I have been employed as a part-time typist and a wages clerk, and we have both worked as shop assistants. Alan has served petrol at week-ends and has occasionally picked up the odd bit of jobbing gardening.

We can manage on an incredibly small income. When the miners were working to rule for a minimum weekly wage of £40, and the talk throughout the country was of £20 being the 'breadline' limit for a married couple—we were managing happily on £9 a week, and running a half-ton van. At the time of writing this, prices are soaring and the miners are talking of a claim for a basic £60 to £65 a week. And what of our financial position? For the last four weeks our total income has been three lamb chops!

15. Y CYMRY

If I were a Welsh-speaking Welshwoman I should probably refuse ever to speak English, and I would be out with my paint-pot at the cross roads with the rest of them, obliterating English place-names. There is no earthly reason why English mis-spellings and translations of Welsh place names should not now be put right. If the Government can muddle all of us by changing the names of our counties, I don't see why they should not put right a few mistakes whilst they are at it. Newport should be Casnewydd, Cardiff is Caerdydd, Denbigh is Dinbych; and let us have no pussy-footing with both names appearing on signposts. Let us just have the correct one—the Welsh one.

I don't go along with the Welsh patriots on their holiday cottage cavorting however. The buying-up of country cottages by wealthy townspeople is not a problem peculiar to Wales. Young penniless couples from Cornwall, the Lake District and Scotland have a similar gripe. The sad break-up of country community life is a curse of the age in which we live, and it is a universal curse. Anyway, if you want to stop local man 'A' from selling a hovel at an inflated price to starry-eyed townsman 'B', then surely 'A' is the man you should go and duff up. It is *his* windows that should be broken, not those of unsuspecting only-wanting-a-bit-of-piece-and-quiet 'B'.

But the passions of Nationalism are strong, unswerving— and understandable. The Welsh have something worth hanging on to.

The survival of the Welsh language is a phenomenon. Historically, the policy of successive British governments has been to eradicate the languages of its Celtic nationals, and

English was the only permitted language in the schools at the turn of the century. The result has been the almost complete disappearance of the local tongue in Ireland and Scotland, but not so in Wales. In spite of being under English domination for nearly seven hundred years, Welsh is still the first language of many of its nationals, especially in the north and midwest. Why? One cannot give as a complete reason the harsh mountainous terrain and isolated communities where the language might have lived on, because the same argument would apply to parts of Ireland and Scotland, as do the national traits of stubborn independence and strong feelings of kinship. I am wondering if, perhaps, the Welshman had a bit more subtleness and guile than his Irish and Scottish brothers. When the Imperialist English conqueror said Thou Shalt Speak English, the Scotsman and the Irishman said 'Like Hell we will,' and picked up their swords to prove it. Whereupon they were struck down by the all-powerful conqueror. But the Welshman did not argue and, whilst craftily appearing to co-operate with the conqueror, in fact went on living his life in exactly the same way as before.

Anyway, whatever the reason, if you come up around these parts you will be made strongly aware that English is a foreign language. It is not normally spoken at all, except to English visitors, and the locals have to make a mental 'change of gear' in order to reassemble their Welsh thoughts into English phrases for the benefit of the strangers. Is it any wonder that the Welsh-speaking Welshman dislikes having to complete English application forms for his vehicle and television licences?

Alan and I accept, without any qualification, that we are foreigners in this land. We are here on sufferance, and we try not to make too many blunders. If our radio programmes, newspapers and official documents were entirely in the Welsh language, we would accept this as being the correct state of affairs—and it would certainly add impetus to our attempts to learn the language.

We realized before we came that it was absolutely essential for us to learn something about the Welsh language, even if we only mastered the basics of pronunciation. To the average

English eye a Welsh place-name is an irritating jumble of impossible letters that the brain can do nothing with. Like Dwygyfylchi. And if that brought you to a stop, you now know what I mean. But place-names crop up in everyday language. One cannot keep jabbing a finger at a map and saying 'that place there', so we started to learn Welsh.

It was not long before we could rattle off all place-names without hesitation and we can now ask the bus times to places like Yspytyifan and Llanllwchaiarn-Iwrch as a matter of course. But our progress with the language since then has been less spectacular. Although Welsh is similar in construction to French, and follows the same rules, it has a most exasperating complication, that of word mutation. The first few letters of any word can change, according to the word that precedes it. For example, the Welsh word for head is *pen*. But 'his head' is '*ei ben*', 'my head' is '*fy mhen*', and 'her head' is '*ei phen*'. Similarly the word for house—'*ty*', can be '*dy*', '*nhy*' or '*thy*', and leg—'*coes*'—can be '*goes*', '*nghoes*' or '*choes*', all of which makes searching for a word in the dictionary a rather frustrating matter because (in our dictionary at any rate) it will only be listed under the original spelling.

And if this wasn't complicated enough, there is the business of local dialects. According to our teacher on the BBC *Welsh for Beginners* programme, the Welsh word for 'now' is '*nawr*'. But the locals will have none of it. They turn it completely backwards, letter by letter. Up in these parts 'now' is '*rwan*'. Our neighbours have confessed that the 'South Wales Welsh' spoken on television sometimes puzzles them and, so far as we are concerned, this different use of words can lead to unfortunate misunderstandings. One day when we were working at the mill, Alan—full of the previous night's Welsh lesson —announced in Welsh his intention of going outside to 'wash'. There was a moment's shocked silence. Faces reddened, mouths dropped open and then, as comprehension dawned, screams of laughter followed the baffled Alan as he left the room. It was many weeks before I could persuade my colleagues to give me an explanation. Alan may have been going outside to 'wash' according to the BBC but, so far as our colleagues at the mill were concerned, he was going outside to do something that just isn't done in polite circles. Or, if it is, it isn't talked about. We have avoided 'washing' in BBC Welsh ever since.

I am now competent to speak Welsh when passing the time of day with my neighbours, and when giving my order at the village shop. But I cannot understand Welsh spoken to me unless it is said very slowly and carefully. This makes conversation very stilted and difficult so, once again, allowances are made for the stranger, and we all lapse into English.

'Making allowances' is something our neighbours have been doing for us ever since we came to Hafod. We hope that our manners have improved slightly, but at first we must have seemed a very insensitive pair of boors.

Take, for example, the business of calling on one's neighbour to buy eggs. In the town, one gets over business at the door as rapidly as possible. This probably stems from a suspicious attitude that is adopted by both the caller and the called upon. When someone knocks at your front door in the City, you approach the door with the words, 'Not today thank you' forming on your lips, and with the idea of slamming the door shut as soon as possible. The caller, knowing this, gabbles out his business as fast as possible before the door is slammed in his face. This ingrained defensive attitude is, I think, the reason why my neighbour barely had time to open her kitchen door before I blurted out the words, 'Have you any eggs?' As neighbourly business is not conducted upon such abrupt lines, this opening remark must have seemed like a slap in the face. Nevertheless, it was always followed up by a kind insistence that I step into the kitchen (no matter how muddy my boots) and a gentle enquiry as to my health, and that of Alan. It has taken several years of contact with Welsh good manners to soften the edges of our City boorishness.

I think that all Welsh people must be born with good manners and a gentle thoughtfulness for other people's welfare. Certainly the kindness that we have been shown by our neighbours suggests this. Their generosity is limitless, and we know that they would rise to the occasion to help someone in difficulties, without thought for themselves. One neighbour has frequently lent us his van, and on several occasions for a week at a time, at—I suspect—considerable inconvenience to himself. Any attempts to pay for such favours are brushed firmly aside. A good deed can only be paid for by another good deed in return. Kindness cannot be paid for by cash. Unfortunately we can never seem to find enough opportunities to return good deeds; in the currency of helpfulness we are continually in debt to our neighbours.

Last December we were away from Hafod and, in a small festive gesture, we invited a few of our neighbours to help themselves in our absence to a Christmas tree each from the plantation. They did so happily. But when we returned we noticed that the plantation appeared to be complete. No tree was missing. 'Oh, we replanted them after Christmas,' we were told. Whilst accepting the gift in principle, they had no intention, apparently, of depriving us of a potential sale!

Yet, in spite of the unstinting friendliness showed to us, we have no illusions of 'belonging'. We live alongside these people, but we are not of them. I think that a Welsh community is so close-knit that a stranger could join it only by marrying into it.

Most of our neighbours have lived all their lives in this area, and they look out over fields, mountains and moorland that has remained largely unchanged for generation after generation. It must be good to repair a stone wall that you know your great-grandfather had built, and to share common rights upon the mountain with your neighbour, whose forefathers shared those same rights with *your* forefathers. What secure feelings of 'belongingness' and continuity this must give you. Herds of the sturdy black Welsh cattle are handed on from father to son, and every evening the cows that graze near Hafod are called in for milking. We cannot see the farm of this neighbour, but we hear his voice calling in the cows. It is truly a call of the mountains: a high, wild chant. Leastways, that's how it sounds to us. For all we know he might be yelling, 'Come on in you lazy sods!' but carrying across the open moor on a summer's evening, the call sounds as old and as mystical as the mountains themselves. The scene could be an upland pasture in any country in the world, and during any century; a man out upon the hills, calling in his cows. Sometimes his wife and daughter fetch them in. Then the cry is high and shrill, but the chant is similar. And it's all the same to the cows. After the first stanza, each gentle head is swung towards home and the beasts carefully lumber their way across the open moor.

Occasionally the dogs are sent out to do the job. We get the impression that they are directed from the back door by shouts and whistles. It all seems very well organized, both dogs and cattle knowing exactly what is required of them.

No wonder that the Welsh hill farmers are a proud and independent bunch. They walk firmly upon this land that is theirs by rights and ancient tradition.

Cycling home through the village one night I saw that there were cars parked near the chapel, and as I approached I heard the sound of singing. At the chapel doors I put one foot to the ground and paused to listen. Accompanied by the harmonium, Welsh voices were rising and falling in sweet harmony. I knew the hymn, and I joined in. At the end of the last verse the harmonium stopped and there was a shuffling of feet. I quickly pedalled away. I like to join in with a bit of hymn singing, but I didn't want to be caught intruding.

No choirs can sing hymns like Welsh choirs. The Welsh sing hymns for pleasure, and as part of their daily life. We sang hymns whilst packing flour at the mill, and children going home from school sing hymns along the road. And surely, only in Wales, would you hear hymns coming from a juke box in a pub!

But it is not only hymns that they sing well—as anyone who has listened to radio and television programmes of 'Welsh Pop' will know. Competitions, talent contests—these are the real stuff of the Welsh singing scene—and the standards are incredibly high. We cannot understand why more 'Welsh Pop' doesn't feature on the national or international *Top of the Pops* programmes. These Welsh youngsters can really sing. Sometimes solo, sometimes in groups, and usually with guitar or harp accompaniment, their songs are melodious, rhythmical, merry, soulful or downright nationalistic—but always sung beautifully.

It is good to see that this Welsh tradition of singing together, in the home, at work and in clubs, is not in the slightest danger of dying out. The original *noson lawen* (merry evening) had a quite practical reason. It was obviously sensible to save on rush lights and turf fires by taking it in turns to gather at each other's firesides in the evening. The recitation of poems, the telling of stories and the singing of songs was the background enjoyment to the homely tasks of carding and spinning wool, knitting and mending. The desire to economize on fuel may have lapsed (although if Society regains its senses it will return) but the *noson lawen* carries on, held more usually now in the village hall or schoolroom. I suspect that the knitting and mending is done these days to the background accompaniment of the television set.

I think, upon reflection, that the Welsh language has survived for the same reason that Welsh individuality has survived. The people of this land have a quietly indomitable and resilient spirit that has lived on through centuries of Dark Age and oppression. This strong awareness of their own national identity is shining as brightly today as it was in the thirteenth century when, under Llywelyn the Great, Wales was at the apex of her power. What's more, I am convinced that should a second Dark Age overtake us ('the crunch' that we are warned is just around the corner) many Welsh rural communities will survive when anarchy, chaos and destruction ravage the rest of 'civilized' Britain.

Not far from here is a tranquil wooded valley lying between the folds of several hills. The valley is drained by a river which alternately roars through boulder-choked gullies, and meanders placidly across the plains on its way down to the broader valley of the Conwy. Within this valley there are two small villages which, at a casual glance, appear to be completely anglicized. The hills have been taken over by the Forestry Commission, the woollen mill is run by people from Yorkshire, and holiday cottages sprout paintily everywhere. Integration between the two races seems total and amicable.

The hotel and pubs are doing very nicely thank you out of tourists, and most cottagers hang out bed and breakfast signs. Colour television sets are now appearing in many households along with the washing machines, refrigerators and oil-fired central heating. Changing the car every twelve months is normal practice.

But this is all on the surface. This is the 'make-up' on the twentieth-century face of the valley. This is the prosperous evidence of Welshmen rising to the occasion. So what happens if 'the crunch' comes, and the English leave the valley, taking with them the well-paid Forestry jobs and fat purses of the tourists? I know what would happen. The people of this valley would shrug their shoulders and take up where they left off a hundred years ago. The technological age was late in coming here, and the people would not have far to reach for their scythes, water pails and chimney-hung cooking pots. The old skills are still here too. The joiner may, today, be fixing laminated plastics to the counter top in the lounge of the hotel, but he knows also how to make privies, plank doors and double-hung sash windows. The native hands that make rockeries and dig gardens for the holiday cottagers also know how to build stone houses and cut slates. I know of two men who are proficient at making spinning wheels, and three women who know how to use them. With fat woolly sheep roaming the hillsides, crops of corn and hay growing in the valley bottom, and turf to be dug upon the moor, the people of these villages will neither starve nor freeze come 'the crunch'. They already have their community life, led by the Minister, the Doctor and the Schoolmaster. The old folk sit and sun themselves upon their doorsteps, and the young take their guitars down to the hall for a *noson lawen*.

Survival in the mountains is something we hear a lot about these days. When parties of inadequately clothed schoolchildren get into difficulties up in the hills because of bad weather, the competence of their leaders is, quite rightly, questioned. What *is* the correct clothing to wear on the mountains? The argument is tossed back and forth between the advocates of man-made fibres and those who champion wool. Some favour canvas tents and bulky blankets, whilst others go for a terylene bivouac and a plastic bag. When Alan and I set out in bad weather we wear several loose layers of cotton and wool, finally topped with a windproof jacket. We are well gloved, booted and wear windproof hoods. We *always* carry waterproof capes and emergency rations of food and drink.

But what does a Welsh hill farmer wear? If one of our neighbours needs to go into the hills during winter, he just gets up from his fireside, pulls on his cap and goes out. He will, of course, be already wearing his wellington boots and may, if the blizzard is really severe, pull on an extra old jacket or raincoat. And how often do you hear of a hill farmer coming to grief in the hills? One very severe winter when all roads were blocked and a blizzard had been raging for several days, a neighbour of ours decided to walk the ten miles across the open moor to Dinbych in order to buy a preparation from the chemist for his baby daughter. The Dinbych moor is a vast and almost featureless plain at the best of times; at the height of a blizzard it must have seemed like Antarctica. With no compass, no extra clothing or food, he set out. When asked to describe the twenty-mile journey he just shrugs his shoulders. He just went to Dinbych, did his shopping and walked home again didn't he? How did he find his way? What sort of ingrained instinct took him safely there and back? He just grins and shakes his head ... And I bet he wasn't even wearing gloves!

16. THE SIMPLE LIFE, ON A PITTANCE

For nine years we have been living in comparative isolation and with very little money upon a windswept moorland in North Wales. What effect has this had upon us?

We are much more aware of natural things—the feel of the wind, the direction of the sun and the movements and sounds of other living things. We move quietly, and when something rustles beside us we remain motionless, turning our eyes and not our heads.

We have become accustomed to living in a perpetual state of insecurity, and this has made us more self-reliant.

Sometimes in winter we have gone for several weeks without seeing anyone else, but only realized it in retrospect; the lack of contact with other people had meant nothing. Indeed, as we are always extremely busy we find unexpected visitors a nuisance. We begrudge the time they take up, and we don't know what to say to them. We have lost the art of making trivial conversation. This happy acceptance of isolation worries us slightly. We could so easily become hermits.

Have we found what we were searching for when we left the city nine years ago? No. But we now realize that the rustic life of our dreams was just an idyll. We are about fifty years too late. One needs to go back in time to escape from the jet planes, car rallies, road 'improvement' schemes and poison sprays—all of which are now part of everyday country life. But we are now learning to accept things as they are, keeping nostalgia for those winter evenings when the kettle is singing upon the hearth and hailstones pound at the window.

Springtime dawns are still exuberant with birdsong, and summer evenings can be tranquil with mystery. We listen with excitement to the first willow-warbler of the year, and watch with astonishment the humming-bird hawk-moth as it moves across the flowering sage bushes. These are moments of pure delight—for all their transience.

Sometimes we feel, rather guiltily, that this is a selfish life we are leading. We are concerned only for each other; our contribution to Society is a very negative one. We do not ask anyone to take away our sewage, bring us water or provide us with electricity. We do almost everything for ourselves—and very little for anybody else. We are in the paradoxical situation of enjoying our isolation, yet feeling the basic human need to be useful members of a community.

Occasionally we are gleefully aware of having cheated the great Industrial Machine that was our true inheritance. We will work diligently for any reasonable employer—but only for a limited time. We have our own interpretation of Gandhi's philosophy of 'enoughness'. We want enough money to live our sort of live—we don't want more than enough. And in living the 'simple life', it is time we are usually short of, not money.

How long can we go on like this? With galloping inflation making nonsense of our carefully thought-out finances, will we be obliged to spend more and more time away from Hafod earning money, in order to spend less and less time upon our much loved patch of land? But that is looking too far ahead, and at Hafod we have learned to live one day at a time.

I sometimes think that the simple life can be led only by someone of independent means, living in a well-appointed town flat, and eating out. One can then leave all the dirty work to someone else whilst one spends the whole day thinking about a poem, or contemplating a rose. And one cannot pass the time more simply than that.

Life at Hafod, on the other hand, is full of complications. We are trying to be largely self-sufficient. This means that we need a great variety of tools, an assortment of materials and lots of ingenuity. We also need plenty of time. Having now organized all these needs, we can manage with very little money.

Unfortunately we are both rather untidy, and a lot of time

is wasted looking for things that weren't where we expected them to be. We keep starting the job of classifying and allocating logical places for all tools, equipment and materials, but it never gets finished. The current job of constructing something may be abandoned in order to attend to an emergency repair; and tools that are required often, tend to be left in the kitchen. When Alan knows that his favourite screwdrivers, saws, planes and chisels are in the corner, and that the shoe repair equipment shares a box with bike parts under the sideboard, he can operate quite efficiently. When he turns over a new leaf and takes it all out to be placed logically in his workshop, he's in danger of not being able to find it next time he wants it.

Keeping ourselves fed, clothed, warm, sheltered and clean seems to take up almost all of our waking hours. The clearest way to describe our activities is to classify them as follows:

Food

The growing, protecting, harvesting, preparing, preserving and storing of food takes up a lot of time. Now that we are growing a wide variety of fruit and vegetables we never have to buy any from the shop, except for potatoes during our 'hungry' period in late spring and early summer when we have eaten all the old ones and the new ones are not yet ready for lifting. Apart from this, and occasional purchases of apples, we live by a philosophy of what fruit and vegetables we cannot grow, we do without.

Our stored root vegetables are usually eaten by April but we always have an abundance of dried peas in stock and they last until pea-picking times comes round again at the end of July. We try to organize things so that there is always something green to go out and pick for dinner—Brussels sprouts, kale, spinach beet, seakale beet, broad bean tops, or turnip tops. For salads we rely heavily on the Hafod natural growth.

The only cultivated salad crops we can grow successfully are beetroot, lettuce, radish and various types of perennial onions that serve as 'spring' onions. None of these is ready for gathering before July at the earliest, yet we are eating plates of salad every other day from April until November, and occasionally in the winter as well. Only during the severest winter weather is it impossible to wander out into the garden at Hafod and find something green to eat raw. Most plants are edible (or so I have read) and many of them apparently contain large quantities of essential vitamins and minerals. Admittedly a lot of them are tasteless but, served up my way, they can be made appetizing. Come with me on a salad-gathering expedition. I wander out into the garden with a large bowl. First I stop to pick a handful of chives, then a few sprigs of spearmint. Yellow rocket is growing on the bank behind the mint, so I have a few leaves. A particularly luscious dandelion growing alongside the path will be gathered up with some sorrel leaves, and then I go into the vegetable garden. It is June and the lettuces and radishes are still too small, so I pick a few leaves from the spinach beet. I then go on to the pond where the wild water mint and peppermint can be gathered (only a few sprigs of the water mint—it is rather sickly in quantity). Nearby grows a handsome crop of chick-weed, and this is a main ingredient in any salad of ours. It grows here almost all the year round. (I have read that it used to be sold commercially as a substitute for watercress.) The patch of pignut is worth investigation. Sometimes at this time of the year I can find quite large 'nuts' beneath these pleasant white flowers, and a few chopped pignuts are a welcome addition to the salad. Then to the herb garden where I gather sage, thyme, parsley, marjoram, lemon balm and several leaves of comfrey. I will also pick off a few blackcurrant, raspberry and strawberry leaves in passing. My bowl is now full. This greenery does not need much washing (there is such an abundance growing that I pick only the best specimens) and I will cut it all up together, with scissors. The pignuts will be scraped and chopped. This is my basic salad. Sometimes I add a handful of sultanas or gooseberries. I then bind it all together with a dessertspoonful of home-made salad cream. The mixture is tasty, juicy and refreshing. We eat it with potatoes (plain boiled if new, otherwise baked in their jackets, mashed or chipped, a tin of pilchards, or hard-boiled eggs and cheese. This represents our main meal of the day for a large part of the year, and we never tire of it. The ingredients of the salad will, of course, change with the season, and a list of the wild food we eat at Hafod is given in Appendix B.

During winter our salads diminish, and sometimes I can find only enough fresh greenery to garnish a cheese sandwich, but we try to find *something* raw to eat every day.

Before we came to Hafod I could identify only the commonest of garden 'weeds'. Alan knew a great deal more, and was able to teach me, and we also have some books to consult. Although there are very few poisonous plants, I never pick any leaf for a salad unless I have positively identified it. Alan is not so fussy and will nibble at anything that he thinks *looks* all right. Meals of salad prepared by him are liable to be full of surprises, but when it is cut up and mixed with salad cream it all looks the same. 'Guess what you've just eaten,' he will say with a leer at the end of the meal.

He claims that his method of selection is just as good as my 'positive' identification—which is suspect anyway. His doubts are, perhaps, justified. Having discovered what I thought was a fine bank of wood sorrel growing near us I ate handfuls of it daily for a week—having read in my herb book that it was good for 'female troubles'. When Alan discovered what I was doing he pointed out that I was munching my way through a crop of wood anemones. Anyway, for what it's worth, I can now record for posterity that eating one handful of wood anemones per day does you no harm whatsoever; neither is it of the slightest value for the relief of 'female troubles'.

We would very much like to believe in herbal cures but, so far, we have not found any that work. I treated a small, but persistent cyst twice a day with the juice of cleavers, over a period of four months. And it made not the slightest difference (except for a dark brown stain over my skin). Eventually, after another eighteen months, the cyst disappeared of its own accord. Elderflowers pressed into Vaseline will produce a soothing ointment for rough hands, we read. It does. But Vaseline without elderflowers is equally effective. Alan is sometimes troubled with eczema and has persisted with blackberry and elder, but has always eventually to resort to the chemist. These are the only disorders we have suffered. We started our herbal 'cures' with faith, and have endeavoured to be persistent. Perhaps it was our diagnosis that was wrong. Anyway, we still believe that somewhere amongst all the folk-lore and whimsy there is a grain of truth about herbal 'cures' but, sadly, we have not discovered any.

We do not make a sacred ritual about this gathering of wild food to eat. Although we are prepared to try anything once, we generally go for only those plants that are easiest to gather and prepare. The more awkward ones we avoid, no matter how good they are supposed to be. Couch-grass for instance. We certainly have masses of it, and it would be very handy if we could eat our way through it, but the first attempt to chew some of the roots convinced us that this was 'starvation' food only. A rich source of mineral nutrients it might be, but ye Gods, you have to work hard to get at them. Nettles are another failure so far as we are concerned. Only the tops of the young ones are said to be palatable; you have to wear gloves to gather them and a bowlful that could take half an hour to pick will boil down into a couple of tablespoonsful of food; and somewhat rough textured tasteless food to boot. A mouthful of wet blotting paper would have much the same feel and taste. So that is one beneficial source of vitamin C that we are likely to do without, unless we are really desperate.

We are both extremely cautious about gathering fungi to eat. Our guide book to mushrooms and toadstools starts with a chapter describing what happens when poisonous fungi are eaten. The description of stomach pains, nervous disorders and the violent convulsions of the body that precede death is enough to make the most earnest wild-food gatherer chuck his collecting bowl over the hedge and settle for fish and chips. So we restrict ourselves to the ones we know—field mushrooms, horse mushrooms, puffballs and chanterelles—and then only when they are very young. Puffballs and chanterelles are delicious with egg and chips, or just fried bread. But for something to get your teeth into nothing equals a horse mushroom. We have picked them so large that one head will fill the frying pan. Alternatively, a large horse mushroom chopped up, fried in butter and thickened with a white sauce, makes a delicious accompaniment to a dish of young boiled potatoes, carrots and peas. One day we might try drying horse mushrooms to add to our winter stores. So far we have always greedily eaten fresh every one that we have picked.

Our home grown winter stores comprise potatoes, swedes, onions, shallots, garlic, marrows and carrots (we dig parsnips and Jerusalmen artichokes as we want them); several large earthenware jars of dried peas, bunches of dried mint, sage, thyme, marjoram and rosemary; jars of beetroot and chutney, pots of jam and bottles of fruit.

Preserving by bottling in jars made for the job can be quite expensive if you allow yourself to be bamboozled by the preserving-jar manufacturers. 'Use once only for preserving' it says on some of my lids. I have two dozen or so that I have been using for five years, and I have never had a failure. Occasionally I will abandon a lid after a couple of years' use if the seal seems badly damaged. But, when in doubt, I will give it another chance, and I have not miscalculated yet. The snap closure and rubber ring method of bottling used to be my favourite, but a few years ago the manufacturers of jam played a dirty trick upon us all. They stopped putting their jam in old-fashioned 1 lb and 2 lb jars, and introduced fancy shapes and sizes of jar that could not be used with the snap closure and rubber ring equipment. Fortunately I still have some of the old-fashioned ones. Moreover, I have found a way of getting back at those unkind jam manufacturers.

Nowadays, honey, jam, peanut butter, etc. is sold in jars that have a plastic seal bonded to the lid. I have found that these jars and lids are perfectly satisfactory for home bottling, and can be used time and time again. This is what I do. I take any such jar and inspect the lid to see that the seal inside is not peeling away from the metal surface. I pack my jar full of fruit, fill it with cold water, then put it (on an old enamelled iron tray) in the bottom oven of the stove and leave it to come up to simmering point. I then transfer it to the top oven for a few minutes to bring the *jar* above boiling point. In the meantime I have placed the lid in a dish and, just as my jar is ready to lift from the oven, I pour boiling water over the lid. I then take my jar from the oven, lift the lid with tongs from the near-boiling water and place it on the jar.

Then, grabbing a tea towel, I screw the lid down hard. As the jar cools, the lid should be drawn inwards. Of course, with this method, you don't have that reassuring 'pop' that tells you all is well. Neither can you 'lift by the lid' to check that your 'vacuum' is there. You just have to go by the look of the thing ... whether or not the lid appears to be sucked down.

Now that we buy honey and peanut butter in bulk I rarely obtain such useful jars over the counter, but I scrounge a few from relatives. I have had failure with one jar only, and that was when a piece of rhubarb was trapped between jar and lid.

In the same fashion I make use of the manufacturer's pickle and chutney jars to bottle beetroot and chutney. The beetroot I treat as I do fruit (using cold vinegar, of course, not water) and I find that this is a much more satisfactory way of keeping beetroot than storing them in dry sand. (In our experience small beetroot always shrivel after a couple of months in sand or earth.) Chutney, of course, does not *have* to be in vacuum-sealed jars, but it will keep for years if it is. When making chutney I put a tray full of empty jars into the bottom oven to heat up, and then pour the hot chutney into them, finally slapping on the lids that have been dunked in boiling water.

I can assure you that these unorthodox methods work—and you have the added delight of getting something for nothing out of the jar makers.

I am rarely able to bottle enough beetroot or make enough chutney to last us through the whole winter, but the fruit and jams always overlap the season. As I write this now, the strawberries are ripening and the gooseberries are almost ready for picking, yet I still have six 2 lb jars of last year's raspberries left in my store cupboard, and several pounds of raspberry, blackcurrant and blackberry jam.

Wild foods from the surrounding countryside always form part of our winter stores, but they cannot be relied upon. One year we picked two large biscuit tins full of hazel nuts; the following year we found only a handful. Blackberries rarely let us down. I am picking them from late August until the end of October and usually have a goodly amount of bramble jelly, blackberry jam and bottled blackberries in stock over the winter. I think I have fathomed the reason for the saying 'Never pick blackberries after the end of September because the Devil has pissed on them.' They definitely lose their flavour as the season dies, and are not to be recommended for jam-making or bottling. (They are liable to be absolutely tasteless after bottling.) So, although I carry on picking blackberries for as long as blackberries are upon the bush, I never preserve them at the tag end of the season. We eat them the same day. (I think, in fact, that it is quite late in the season when the Devil comes pissing up here, because it has to be nearly November before our blackberries deteriorate.) Whinberries are another delicious wild fruit to be gathered. But you have to be very patient. Two of us picking whinberries all afternoon will only produce enough fruit for a pie and a couple of jars. But the exquisite flavour of whinberry pie is worth a few afternoons' work in the sun.

Most of our protein* is obtained from eggs, cheese and pulses. Occasionally in winter I buy stewing beef or neck of lamb to add to a stew, but we never have roast meat unless Alan comes home with a joint as payment for a job.

Coffee, tea, wholemeal, white flour, oatmeal, honey, and a few other things we buy in bulk. It amazes us that it costs less to have these things delivered to our doorstep from the south of England than it would if we went to buy them in Llanrwst. Bread, cakes and biscuits we make for ourselves.

There is a lot of mumbo-jumbo written about breadmaking. There is nothing precise or scientific about the procedure, and quantities of yeast, flour and water can be varied without the finished product varying much. And we have never found the rising dough sensitive to cold. Indeed, my early failures at bread-making were due to taking too much notice of all those warnings about cold draughts, and I was putting my dough to rise in too warm a place; the yeast was being killed off before the loaves reached the oven. We usually use a mixture of wholemeal and white flour. This produces a lighter and cheaper loaf than if it were made of pure wholemeal. We prefer the coarser textured, compost grown, stone-

* I am making free with an accepted nutritional concept here. I wouldn't recognize a protein if I saw one.

ground wholemeal, although we do not believe even half of the nutritional claims made by the packers. We are sceptical about anything that comes out of a packet, especially when it bears a 'healthfood' label. It is just that we like the bits of bran and grain you find in the coarser stuff. However, the trouble with compost-grown wholemeal is that you are liable to find bits of the compost in it. I have sifted maggots, mice droppings and straw from mine on occasions. But unless you are able to grow and grind your own corn you have to settle for white flour tainted by chemicals or wholemeal possibly tainted by animals. Take your choice. Either way you will probably produce a tastier loaf than any you could buy.

Fuel

Our solid-fuel stove provides most of the heat in the cottage all the year round. It also provides the cooking facilities and the hot water. It works very efficiently upon 1¼ to 1½ cwt per week of the cheapest coal available. This, undoubtedly, is one of the main reasons why we can live on such a small income at Hafod. We find it cheaper to buy our coal from England. A 9 to 10 ton lorry load from Crewe costs less than half as much as the local coal. (At present we are coming to the end of some rubbish that cost us 45p per cwt.) So you can see that once we have had a load of coal delivered we know that our main fuel bill has been paid for the following three years.

We have rights of turbary upon part of the moor and every year we dig turf to enjoy on the parlour fire. We cannot dig very much because the peat bog is half a mile distant, and wet turf is very difficult to cart away. Ideally, one should dig it and leave the turves to drain—going up every now and then to turn them. This is how it used to work in the old days. But people are not so honest now, and visiting motorists who park and picnic upon the moor will steal any dug turf left there (or even bring spades and dig it themselves)—so the digging of our turf each year is, more or less, merely a gesture to maintain our rights.

We also burn wood upon the parlour fire. We have two elderly ash trees and a wych-elm that usually present us with a few boughs after a gale, and, of course, twiggery galore. Most of our kindling comes from the woody stalks of plants that have been left to die standing. The late autumn growth of nettles, knapweed, golden rod, marguerites and great willow-herb, etc., are never chopped down. By the end of winter they stand up, parched, crackling and stiff, ready to be snapped off. We amass great bundles of it in outhouses and it makes marvellous kindling. Even better than these stalks are the dead stems of Jerusalem artichokes. We made the mistake one year of trying to compost the bamboo-like stems of Jerusalem artichokes, but they just refused to rot. Since then we just leave them lying around on the ground all winter and they dry off to become completely hard and crisp. One thoroughly dried Jerusalem artichoke stalk is enough kindling for two days' parlour fires.

Although our electric lighting is comparatively expensive it is always paid for well in advance. Having, say, just bought a new battery we know that we shall have no more to pay for our electricity until eighteen months' time when we replace the three years old one. There is no worry about a quarterly bill coming along. That is the trouble with having the mains supply, once you are hooked up to it you are hooked for ever, and even if you went without electricity entirely there would still be a bill to pay each quarter. This complete independence is, perhaps, the main delight in owning a windcharger. We know that we are likely to be without electricity if the wind does not blow for a fortnight or more, or if the batteries are in so bad a condition that they will not hold the charge. But this state of affairs does not come about suddenly. We are never caught napping. When the hydrometer readings drop below the half-charge mark we will decide not to use electric light any more until the batteries get a fresh charge from the wind. This means that we can go on using the radio (which takes very little current) but we get out the paraffin lamps for lighting.

We have always been free and easy with paraffin. If the Wellstood stove is a bit sluggish I will light the Primus to make toast, or get the chip-pan boiling. When I use my clothes boiler the $\frac{1}{2}$ gallon Primus will be roaring away for about half an hour, and we also use paraffin for cleaning machinery. In this fashion we have been getting through about 20 gallons of paraffin a year. With the current soaring prices we shall obviously have to use this fuel more sparingly. (In 1965 a gallon of white paraffin cost us 1s 7d. In 1974 it is unobtainable here and we have to buy a coloured variety at 30p per gallon. We cannot get any reduction in price on less than 300 gallons, which we couldn't have delivered anyway.)

Transport

In my opinion the best way of progressing from A to B is to walk. The second best way is to cycle. Alan feels the same, only in reverse order. Our physiques differ accordingly. When Alan, lithe and graceful, climbs onto his machine he becomes part of it; a picture of slim, spinning, curving, swishing movement. You will find me pounding along behind him and, having taken one glance at me in shorts, you will agree that these legs were meant for walking.

Our boots and cycles take us everywhere. Our rucksacks and cycle bags carry paraffin, groceries, paint, plaster, ironmongery, library books, etc. ... but there *are* limits. If we want a hundredweight bag of cement, or a roll of wire netting, and have no vehicle we are in trouble. No shop in Llanrwst will agree to deliver a few odd items to an off-beat place like Hafod and we have, on occasions, had to rely on the generosity of neighbours. We do not like *modern* motor vehicles, and we do not like motoring. But it is no use sitting in splendid isolation upon our hillside pontificating about the evils of this motorized age when there is no way of getting our bag of cement up from Llanrwst other than by somebody's motor vehicle. At one time we did briefly consider buying a horse and cart but decided that taking it out on the main road would amount to cruelty. So, from time to time over the past few years, we have been owners of some form of utility vehicles. But no vehicle of ours has ever had much use. It spends most of its time just sitting around, blotting the landscape.

All stoves, lamps and machinery (e.g. cycles, mangle, type-writer, sewing machine, motor vehicle) are regularly checked over by Alan and parts are replaced when necessary. If a part needs replacing and we have been unable to get a spare, Alan will improvise, or even make a new part. Anything that breaks, or wears out, will normally be repaired. Alan has repaired galvanized iron wash-tubs and jugs, the firebox door and cleaning tools of Stove, kettles, saucepans, furniture, shoes and wellington boots. (Wellington boots very rarely wear out, they split across the instep or get punctured. Alan repairs them with cycle patches outside and linen inside. Sometimes it takes ten or more patches to repair one split successfully.)

For Alan to fail to repair a broken object is rare, although he usually starts by declaring the thing unrepairable. 'I can't do anything with this', he will say, tossing some broken object aside, 'it's had it'. But later I will come into the kitchen and find him sitting there with the thing in his hand. He is looking at it, and is lost in thought and I know that the repair job is now under way. If it is made of wood, metal, stone, rubber or leather, then it can be repaired. If it is made of plastics then (according to Alan) it cannot. A large plastic ewer with a small split in it is an object of much chagrin to Alan. One tiny fracture, and the thing is useless. It ought not to be allowed!

The repair of things made of cloth is generally my concern. When Alan's shirt collars fray I turn them. When they fray again I make a new collar out of the tail. By then the back of the shirt will be wearing thin. When it splits I replace the whole back with the front of another shirt whose back has split also. Trousers are patched at the knees and also the back-side. Patches appear upon patches that are, in their turn, upon patches. I knit all our pullovers and socks, and they are darned indefinitely. When a pullover becomes so darned and shapeless that it is no longer comfortable, I cut away the darned bits (and compost them) and unravel what I can of the remaining wool. This will be used to darn other pullovers. Both of us look, for much of the time, like beings left behind on Robinson Crusoe's island. We have a few respectable clothes for public appearances, but at Hafod our only concern is to be comfortable. Alan is sometimes critical of my repair work. Did I have to repair his blue overalls with a green patch sewn with pink cotton? I know that his repairs are always neat and unobtrusive, but then, I work to different principles. If I have a lot of green cloth, and there is more pink cotton than any other and I have no particular use for pink cotton ... then these are the materials that I will use for patching. And what the devil does it matter what his overalls look like anyway?

We buy quite a lot of our clothes from ex-Government stores. They are very good value for money. In fact, the only place these days where you will find a bit of good quality wool worsted or serge is in a pair of army trousers or a W.R.A.C. skirt. Army angola shirts last five times longer than any civilian types, and the army combat jackets are ideal for wearing in wind and rain.

Cutting each other's hair hardly counts as 'repair' work, but I suppose it could be called 'maintenance'. It certainly saves us a lot of money anyway; not to mention time. We bought a do-it-yourself kit of scissors, clippers and a comb in 1963 (two years before we came to Hafod) and neither of us has been inside a hairdresser's establishment since.

Tax and Insurance

We have discovered the one absolutely infallible method of beating the tax man. Our earnings never approach the taxable level. Our only worry is that the tax man will not believe us. Like gypsies, hippies and other non-conformists we are not at ease when dealing with the Authorities. There is mutual distrust.

As our income is well below the normally accepted 'bread-line' we felt justified in applying for a rates rebate. But when it came to completing the column 'income over the past five weeks' we decided that entering 'half a shoulder of lamb, 3 dozen bantam eggs, 6 fencing posts and £37.50 cash' wasn't going to get us anywhere. So we worked out a cash equivalent and entered it. But, even so, as a 'self-employed' man Alan is supposed to produce 'proof' of earnings. We decided against trying to cook up some 'proof' and so his statement of earnings goes unsupported. I can see that our application is doomed to failure.

Alan's earnings are so low that he is allowed to put the 'non-employed' stamp upon his National Insurance card. But, even so, the Authorities are not giving much away. He has to find £1.90 each week for this stamp at the time of writing, and increases always seem to be looming on the horizon.

Leisure activities

Apart from buying the occasional glass of beer (and very rarely a gramophone record, book or film) we spend no money upon entertainment. We listen to our records and the radio (that's when all the sewing, patching and knitting goes on), and we read. During the winter months we bring home about twelve books a fortnight from the mobile library. The rest of the year we read only about four a fortnight. 'Going out' means, to us, a $1\frac{1}{2}$ hour walk across the fields and through the lanes to the pub; a day out upon the moor with rucksacks, field-glasses and sandwiches; or a day's run on the bikes.

This is not ideal cycling country. We spend a lot of time freewheeling downhill (wearing out the pawls and springs of many freewheels) or grinding in bottom gear uphill (remorse-lessly carving away the sprockets and chair-ring). The sort of cycling beloved of all cyclists—bowling along through pleasant lanes in undulating countryside—is not to be found around here. Nevertheless we cycle, in all seasons of the year.

According to Alan, the bicycle is mechanical perfection. When man invented the bicycle he reached the peak of his attainments. Here was a machine of precision and balance for the convenience of man. And (unlike subsequent inventions for man's convenience) the more he used it, the fitter his body became. Here, for once, was a product of man's brain that was entirely beneficial to those who used it, and of no harm or irritation to others. Progress should have stopped when man invented the bicycle.

The fact that my attitude to the bicycle is something less than total reverence is the cause of much pain to Alan. The careless way in which I prop it against a wall, or drop it into a hedge makes him wince. But I can't see any difference between my propping and dropping and his—no matter how many times he demonstrates. And apparently I do not ride it properly either. I am always being urged to 'ankle', to 'ride' the bumps and to use alternate brakes when making a long descent. And my gear changing sets his teeth on edge.

Any repair job is an excuse to have a machine in bits. Parts are handled lovingly and my admiration is sought for the solidity of our Campagnolo gears, the lightweight strength of our Constrictor Conloy (Standard) Asp rims, or the silkiness of my pre-war Bayliss Wiley steel hub. But his most devoted worship is reserved for his Blumfield large flange light alloy hubs. They are smoothed and polished, and a wheel is spun whilst he watches in dreamy fascination. He is always 'improving' the bikes. Little modifications are carried out—oilways are drilled, and seals and nipples fitted, rough surfaces and sharp edges eliminated, alignments and adjustments checked, wheels trued and balanced—all to make an easier, smoother ride, or simply in his desire to achieve mechanical perfection.

Obtaining the 'correct' riding position is of great importance to Alan. I would not mind betting that if his brake levers were moved one-sixteenth of an inch he would be complaining of backache within half a mile and everything would have to stop whilst he readjusted things. This is all very well, but he is constantly trying to find *my* 'correct' riding position too. He will sometimes decide that I look too stretched out, or hunched up, and will alter the angle of bends and saddle. He will move the saddle up, down, back or forward, and tilt it at several different angles, each time asking me, 'Is that better?' Not only am I not aware that it needed bettering, I don't notice that he has moved anything. No wonder he despairs.

Nevertheless, I still enjoy cycling, in my own insensitive chugging along sort of way, and we have had some good days out on the bikes. And, so long as we have the strength to push the pedals around, it will be our main way of getting about.

Once, on a hot summer's day we were resting at the top of a hill on the 'old' road not far out of Colwyn Bay. With the bikes leaning up against a farm gate, we were sitting at the roadside munching apples. The scent of wild rose and honeysuckle filled the air and the sounds of summer were all around us. I felt absolutely in my right element. I was not just living through a summer's afternoon—I was part of it. Suddenly a car came round the bend and drove on towards Colwyn Bay. A woman looked out of the side window and for an instant our eyes met. We would have been about the same age. I imagined what it must have felt like to be her, sitting inside that car—all clean, tidy, nylon-tighted and upright, with the hot interior-car smell of fumes and warm plastic. What would they do when they got to Colwyn Bay? She would get stiffly out of the car, straighten her dress and find her handbag. They would walk around for a bit, go into a café and have tea, and then drive home. I lay back in the grass; I was dusty, sweaty and absolutely content. I would not, under any circumstances, wish to change places with that woman. And she, looking out at me sitting on my backside at the edge of the road, probably felt exactly the same.

Winter cycling brings its own excitements. Roads coated with ice or blocked with snowdrifts represent a challenge to Alan and he takes a smug delight in being out and about in conditions that bring motoring to a stop. I share his pleasure, but am not really sure why we take the bikes along too. When you are spending half your time lifting them over snowdrifts there doesn't seem a lot of point in having them. But this boots-versus-the-bikes argument is a regular one in this household.

One result of all this winter cycling is that Alan has to work overtime as a mechanic. Slushy salt-laden roads cause severe rusting inside freewheels, despite twice-daily oiling, and we can never dry the machines overnight in these conditions. We have each broken a gear-change mechanism (*not* Campagnolo) in freezing conditions, with snow falling, owing to the ice build up on sprockets and chain.

Riding a bicycle upon ice-glazed surfaces requires a certain clownish skill and a dare-devil attitude to the possibility of collapsing in a heap in the road. Fortunately there is little other traffic in these conditions, and we are so well padded with clothes that such tumbles do not hurt much. One January we were up on the common on our bikes. The approach to the cattle-grid is on a slight downhill gradient. I was leading the way and, too late, I noticed that each metal girder of the grid was coated with ice. Joggling across this grid was a spine-shaking performance in the best of conditions. But is it possible to 'joggle' over ice? I was about to find out. I knew that I should come off if I braked, so settled for a burst of speed instead. As my front wheel met the first ice-laden girder the world slipped away from under my backside. The bike went flying across the road one way, and I went the other. Alan, having stopped in time, came scrabbling anxiously across the grid, his face wide-eyed in alarm. He picked up the bike and examined it carefully. 'You've bent the bloody crank!' he said indignantly, glaring down at me as I lay sprawled in the road ...

Sometimes I can persuade him to leave the bikes at home and we go walking. This is surely some of the finest walking country in Europe. The great wilderness of moorland behind the cottage is at its best in high summer, when the larks are soaring and the heather is in bloom. Here one can walk all day without seeing another living person. The Dinbych moorland is high rolling country without many natural features, but we have come across curiously remote mineshafts and quarry workings, and there is a sprinkling of ruined cottages and farmhouses. No one lives upon the high moor now, and a strange, wistful melancholy hangs about the abandoned homesteads. This land of Hiraethog is well named.

The countryside to the front of the cottage, tumbling down to the Conwy Valley, has an entirely different feeling. Steeply sloping, tiny walled fields, copses of ancient oaks, and helter-skelter streams—this area has supported a scattered community of people continuously for the past few thousand years. The remains of neolithic structures lie about these hillsides, their great gaunt stones scattered secretly amongst the scrubby tangles of blackthorn and hawthorn. One eighteenth-century householder kept his horses in the covered chamber of a nearby neolithic tomb, and subsequent local opportunists have used these handy stones for gateposts, field walls and houses.

In every sunlit glade and upon every bracken-covered slope there is a strong presence of the past—a past that stretches back into misty timelessness, and yet is here right with you now. Two thousand years before Christ, men were tugging at the stones upon these hillsides, and men are still at it now. You can come across them in their shirt sleeves, sweating profusely as they heave a stone into position when repairing a wall or repositioning a gatepost. Century after century of men's hands upon the stones. It gives a feeling to the place.

We have walked these wooded slopes in the drowsy warmth of a summer's afternoon, when the low hanging boughs of birch and oak almost meet the hedge parsley and foxgloves, and the hum and whirr of insects fills the air. We have also crunched through them on snow-wrapped winter's days when the land is muffled and silent.

These winter walks are short ones, because we like to be back at Hafod before darkness falls. Climbing up from the valley in the dusk of a winter's afternoon, we are aware of a hushed stillness falling across the hills. The mountains, with shawls of snow around their lofty shoulders, are lit by the afterglow and a cold winter moon climbs into the sky over the moor. As we walk up over the last hillock we know that the cottage will come into view. When we reach the top the whole vast moorland snowscape is spread before us; wild, lonely and strange. And there, in the middle distance, we see the cottage. I know that there is a beef stew in the bottom oven, and the kitchen will be warm with the smell of it. We stride happily onwards, the snow crunching and squeaking beneath our boots. Hafod is a good place to come home to.

THE END

APPENDIX A. THE HAFOD BIRD LIST

(Listed in order of their scientific classification, according to P. A. D. Hollom's *Popular Handbook of British Birds*.)

Birds nesting successfully in or near the buildings

Partridge
Skylark
Swallow
House martin
Carrion crow
Great tit
Blue tit
Wren
Mistle-thrush

Song thrush
Blackbird
Wheatear
Whinchat
Redstart
Robin
Whitethroat
Willow warbler
Hedge sparrow

Meadow pipit
Pied wagtail
Starling
Goldfinch
Linnet
Redpoll
Chaffinch
House sparrow

Others—seen from the kitchen windows

Heron
Canada goose
Shelduck
Mallard
Buzzard
Marsh Harrier
Hen Harrier
Merlin
Kestrel
Pheasant
Lapwing
Golden plover
Snipe
Curlew
Dunlin
Lesser black-backed gull

Herring gull
Black-headed gull
Wood pigeon
Cuckoo
Barn owl
Little owl
Short-eared owl
Swift
Green woodpecker
Great spotted wood-pecker
Lesser spotted woodpecker
Raven
Hooded crow
Rook
Jackdaw

Magpie
Jay
Treecreeper
Fieldfare
Song thrush
Ring ouzel
Stonechat
Blackcap
Garden warbler
Goldcrest
Pied flycatcher
Tree pipit
Bullfinch
Brambling
Yellowhammer
Reed bunting
Tree sparrow

APPENDIX B. WILD FOOD EATEN, IN SEASON, AT HAFOD

(Each section listed in order of merit, i.e. bearing in mind ease of gathering, preparation and palatability.)

Leaves: chickweed, comfrey, dandelion, raspberry, groundsel, round-leaved mint, horse mint, sorrel, primrose, great plantain, jack-by-the-hedge, borage (introduced), blackberry, lady's smock, nipplewort, sowthistle, chicory, common yellow rocket, strawberry, wood sorrel, water mint. (All eaten raw.)

Flowers: red clover, white clover, borage, wood sorrel, primrose, violet. (All eaten raw.)
elder. (Used only for flavouring gooseberries.)

Fruits: blackberry, whinberry,* raspberry, strawberry, rowanberry. (All eaten either raw, or cooked, except for rowanberry which is used only for making jelly.)

Nuts: hazel, beech. (Eaten raw or cooked. Chopped nuts are delicious in biscuits.)

Roots: pignut. (Eaten raw.)

Fungi: horse mushroom, field mushroom, chanterelle, puffball. (Eaten cooked.)

All the above are growing at Hafod or in the lanes nearby, and they represent only a small part of the total number of wild foods available in Britain. In a gentler climate a much greater variety could be found. Whether they are eaten raw or cooked is largely a matter of personal choice.

* *Vaccinium myrtillus.*

Birds heard from the kitchen, but not identified visually

| Red grouse | Whimbrel | Grasshopper |
| Corncrake | Tawny owl | warbler |

Many more species of bird are within three miles of us (but one or two hundred feet lower) and we are disappointed never to see at Hafod the dippers, greenfinches, nuthatches, chiff-chaffs, grey wagtails, long-tailed tits and redwings that are to be found, from time to time, just down the lane.

GARDEN IN THE HILLS by ELIZABETH WEST

Is the latest account of the adventures, trials, joys and rewards of Elizabeth and Alan West's life in their farmhouse in a remote corner of Wales.

In her familiarly lively style, Elizabeth West describes how they make a garden on a windswept moorland, one thousand feet above sea level, how they battle with storms, blizzards, floods and sheep and tells of their eventual success in growing herbs, fruit and vegetables. You are even invited to try some of Elizabeth's recipes – straight from her primitive but cheerful and homely kitchen!

But *Garden in the Hills* ends on a rather sad note as Mrs West tells of the encroachment of the modern world that threatened to destroy their happy, traditional way of life . . .

0 552 11707 2 – £1.25

THE COMPLETE BOOK OF SELF-SUFFICIENCY
by JOHN SEYMOUR

The Complete Book of Self-Sufficiency is a book for all seasons. Whether you live in town or country, on a farm or in a cottage, in a house with a garden or a flat with a window-box, this book has something for you.

If you want to bake your own bread, brew your own beer, make your own cheese, pickle your own onions, this book will show you how.

If you want to make hay, milk a cow, smoke a ham, design a dairy, convert to solar energy, this book will show you how.

If you want to grow your own vegetables, bottle your own fruit, dry your own herbs, this book will demonstrate exactly what to do.

The Complete Book of Self-Sufficiency is an invaluable manual, packed with illustrations, and every illustration tells its own story, shows you what you need and how to do it.

John Seymour is everywhere recognised as the expert in self-sufficiency. He has lived the life for twenty years, and here he gathers all the expertise he has acquired into one authoritative volume.

0 552 98051 X — £5.95

JOLLY SUPERLATIVE by JILLY COOPER

More witty words and caustic comments from the witheringly funny Jilly Cooper!

With her insatiable love of puns and her vivid response to people and places, JOLLY SUPERLATIVE includes more hilarious happenings in the life of Jilly Cooper – such as the revolt of the Putney Common dogwalkers and a trip to Butlins with 450 vicars! Jilly comments on adultery, suburban snobbery and the sexual rites of professional-class society – as well as the hilarities, horrors and joys of life.

0 552 11801 X – £1.25

SARAH WHITMAN by DIANE PEARSON

A 'God is an Englishman' kind of novel – about a very human kind of Englishwoman, a woman who fought her way up from domestic service to schoolmistress and whose life was touched by three men, one who taught her what it was to love and be loved, another who waited for her in vain, and a third – the strange tormented man who was to be her destiny.

Rich in adventure, history and human passions, this is a novel of astonishing breadth . . . an enthralling panorama of life and love between the wars . . .

'The very stuff of reality . . . SARAH is superb.' Norah Lofts.

0552 09140 5 – £1.95

A SELECTED LIST OF BIOGRAPHIES
AND
AUTOBIOGRAPHIES PUBLISHED
BY CORGI BOOKS

WHILE EVERY EFFORT IS MADE TO KEEP PRICES LOW, IT IS SOMETIMES NECESSARY TO INCREASE PRICES AT SHORT NOTICE. CORGI BOOKS RESERVE THE RIGHT TO SHOW NEW RETAIL PRICES ON COVERS WHICH MAY DIFFER FROM THOSE PREVIOUSLY ADVERTISED IN THE TEXT OR ELSEWHERE.

THE PRICES SHOWN BELOW WERE CORRECT AT THE TIME OF GOING TO PRESS (APRIL '83).

All these books are available at your book shop or newsagent, or can be ordered direct from the publisher. Just tick the titles you want and fill in the form below.

CORGI BOOKS, Cash Sales Department, P.O. Box 11, Falmouth, Cornwall.

Please send cheque or postal order, no currency.

Please allow cost of book(s) plus the following for postage and packing:

U.K. Customers—Allow 45p for the first book, 20p for the second book and 14p for each additional book ordered, to a maximum charge of £1.63.

B.P.F.O. and Eire—Allow 45p for the first book, 20p for the second book plus 14p per copy for the next seven books, thereafter 8p per book.

Overseas Customers—Allow 75p for the first book and 21p per copy for each additional book.

NAME (Block Letters) ....

ADDRESS ....:...............

....